CO-AUL-614

Robert J. Dean

FIRST CORINTHIANS FOR TODAY

BROADMAN PRESS

NASHVILLE, TENNESSEE

Library of Congress Catalog Card Number: 72-79165

Dewey Decimal Classification: 227.2

Printed in the United States of America

CONTENTS

1 A Book for Today   **5**

THE CHALLENGE OF THE CITIES
GETTING ALONG WITHOUT GOD?
PROBLEMS OF A CITY CHURCH

2 Man's Oldest Problem   **26**

OUR PROBLEM WITH OURSELVES (1:10–17)
GOD'S WAY AND MAN'S WAY (1:18–31)
SPIRITUALLY RETARDED CHRISTIANS (2:1 TO 3:4)
LIVING OUTSIDE OURSELVES (3:5 TO 4:21)

3 The Sexual Revolution   **55**

A CONSPIRACY OF SILENCE (5:1 TO 6:11)
WHY SEXUAL IMMORALITY IS WRONG (6:12–20)
SEX AND MARRIAGE (7:1–40)

4 When Is a Man Free?   **84**

HOW FREE AM I? (8:1–13)
WHAT ABOUT MY RIGHTS? (9:1–27)
WHEN FREEDOM BECOMES DANGEROUS (10:1–33)

5 What About the Church?   **106**

WHAT IS THE LIFE OF THE CHURCH? (11:1–34)
WHAT IS THE CHURCH? (12:1–31)
WHEN IS A CHURCH SUCCESSFUL? (13:1–13)
WHEN IS A CHURCH SPIRITUAL? (14:1–40)

6 The Sting of Death   **135**

IF CHRIST BE NOT RISEN (15:1–19)
THE HOPE OF FUTURE RESURRECTION (15:20–34)
VICTORY OVER DEATH (15:35–58)

Notes   **156**

1 A Book for Today

Several years ago, Kenneth Chafin was teaching the book of 1 Corinthians to a group of students in a church camp. The students were bored and disinterested by the opening study on divisions in the church. The topic for the second day's study was discipline in the church. Dr. Chafin wisely began with a modern-life situation that clothed the problem of 1 Corinthians 5 in modern garb. He told the story as if it were a real problem being faced by a local church: A man's wife had died. The man then proceeded to break up his son's marriage. Then he married his son's former wife, his own former daughter-in-law. Dr. Chafin asked the young people what the church should do about this problem involving members of their own congregation.

This brought the students to life. They all were interested in expressing their opinions. Some were resentful that the teacher would even suggest that the church should do anything about the situation. After everyone had had his say, Dr. Chafin read what Paul wrote about a similar situation in Corinth. Dr. Chafin reports what happened then: "To my amazement, while before I read the passage they were a bit upset with me, afterwards they were upset with Paul *and* me. Afterwards one young man came around and made this confession. 'I have always said that I believed everything in the Bible. But today I realized that the reason I can so easily say that is that I do not know everything in the Bible and I have not tried to apply it to life.' "[1]

This is a particularly apt story since this book is about

1 Corinthians. And it is about not only what 1 Corinthians meant to Paul and the Corinthians but also what it means to us today. The approach taken here will begin with the historical setting and meaning of 1 Corinthians, but it will move beyond this to the meaning and application of 1 Corinthians for life in today's world. Probably no book in the Bible touches so many areas of modern life as 1 Corinthians does. Therefore, this practical New Testament book can instruct us and challenge us where we actually live.

But before we turn to the text of 1 Corinthians, let us look at some introductory matters involved in the study of this letter—the city of Corinth, the way the gospel came to Corinth, the problems in the Corinthian church, and the basic material in the letter. If we dare to look, we can see many parallels to modern life even in these background areas.

The Challenge of the Cities

In the days of our founding fathers, America was a rural nation. In 1790 only 5 percent of the population lived in cities. America continued to be basically a rural nation throughout the nineteenth century, but industry caused a gradual shift from the farm to the city. By 1900 the nation was 40 percent urban. During this century the trend has continued. By 1960, 70 percent of the population lived in cities. The 1970 census revealed 73½ percent of the population in metropolitan areas.

Urbanization is going on throughout the world. The rate in many lands is even more rapid than in our own. In Africa, for example, the number of people living in cities of one hundred thousand increased by 629 percent during the first half of this century. By the end of the century the world population will be about six billion. Sixty percent of these six billion people will be living in cities. This means that by A.D. 2000, the urban population of the world will be as large as the entire world population in 1970.

Urban sprawl. In our own land, the growing urban areas will merge together into vast metropolitan sprawls. Some experts claim that by 1985, two thirds of America's population will live on 10 percent of the land area. This 10 percent of the land will be located in four vast urban areas. The first and most crowded runs along the eastern seaboard from Boston to Washington. A second area edges the Great Lakes from Buffalo to Chicago, reaching north to Minneapolis and south to St. Louis. A third area is the rapidly growing West Coast from San Francisco through Los Angeles to San Diego. The fourth urban sprawl borders the Gulf of Mexico from Texas to Florida.

These facts are impressive proof that rural America is no more. The America of Currier and Ives lingers only in memories. Even the shrinking minority of people who live in the country think and act increasingly like city people. The mobility of modern society carries the farmer more often into the city. And the city reaches out to him through the influence of urban-controlled radio and television.

One Christian writer looking realistically at these facts observed: "No one can predict the outcome of the American adventure, but it will be settled in the city. That is where the people are now, and where they're going to be found in the future."[2]

This is not the first age in which cities have played an important role. Cities played a vital role in the first Christian century. Greco-Roman civilization centered around certain key cities. The history of Rome itself involved a shift from farms to cities in a way similar to what has happened in our land. In the early days of the Roman Republic, most people lived and worked on small farms. But by the time of the Empire, a change had occurred: "There was a constant drift to the cities, partly because of the decline in agriculture and small proprietorship, partly from ampler opportunities of making a fortune when commerce became brisk, partly for the sake of adventure, and other causes. The cities afforded ample means of amusement and excitement, as much sought then as now."[3]

The places mentioned in the book of Acts sound like a roll call of some of the greatest cities of the first century—Antioch, Athens, Corinth, Ephesus, Rome. Paul's missionary strategy was to go to the great urban centers of his day. As a result, the churches mentioned in the New Testament were city churches. This surely says something to us about the relevance of the New Testament for our modern age.

Metropolitan Corinth. Corinth was one of the cities visited by Paul. At that time, Corinth was an important metropolitan center with a population of over half a million people. Like many of the cities of America, Corinth was a relatively new city in the middle of the first century when Paul was there. The oldest buildings were little more than a century old. The site itself had been occupied before. Actually, there were two Corinths in ancient history. The former Corinth flourished in the days of Greece's ancient glory, along with Athens and Sparta. But Corinth made the mistake of getting into a war with the vigorous and militant Romans. The city was finally captured, and in 146 B.C. ancient Corinth was completely destroyed. The men were killed; the women and children were sold as slaves. The site lay desolate for a century. Then shortly before his death, Julius Caesar ordered Corinth to be rebuilt as a colony of Rome.

One of the reasons for Caesar's decision was the strategic location of Corinth. It was situated on the narrow isthmus that connects the Greek mainland with the large peninsula of Peloponnesus. This was a key commercial location. The voyage around Cape Malea at the southern end of the Greek peninsula was long and dangerous. Greek sailors had a saying about this voyage, "Let him who sails around Malea first make his will." Therefore, Corinth became the focal point of an east-west trade route. Large ships carried their goods to the isthmus of Corinth. The goods were unloaded and hauled the few miles across the isthmus. Then they were loaded aboard another ship. If the ship was not too large, the ship itself was hauled across the isthmus. A special ship road called a *diolkos* ("haul-across") was used for this unique means of transportation. Several years after Paul's visit, Nero ordered a canal built across the isthmus, but it was not completed. (A canal was built in modern times.)

Corinth's location was a key factor in making it the most important city of Greece in the first century. Athens was still the center of culture and philosophy. But Corinth was the center of commerce and industry. Archaeologists have uncovered the remains of a bronze factory. Corinth also specialized in manufacturing pottery and tile. And shipbuilding also flourished in this seaport town.

Politically, Corinth was the capital of the Roman province of Achaia. The Roman proconsul resided there. (Gallio, the proconsul is mentioned in Acts 18:12.) When Corinth was rebuilt, it was colonized by Romans, many of them veterans. But soon many Greeks also moved to Corinth. And because of its location, Corinth soon attracted people from all over the ancient world. These included Jews and people from other eastern countries. As a result, no city in the ancient world was any more cosmopolitan than Corinth.

Slavery was one of the factors that brought so many nationalities to ancient Corinth. One estimate of the population sets it at 600,000. Of these, probably 460,000 were slaves. The slaves were from all nations. Many of them were talented and cultured people. War was one means of recruiting slaves. Entire populations of defeated nations were sold into slavery. This was at least an advance over a former stage of history when all prisoners were put to the sword. This vast host of slaves from all over the world helped to make Corinth a real "melting pot" of people.

Like cities of all ages, Corinth had its places of entertainment. Athletic events were popular. The Isthmian games were held nearby every other year. These games were second in importance only to the Olympian games held every fourth year. In addition to the usual track events, the games included wrestling, boxing, and chariot racing. Corinth had an outdoor theater with a seating capacity of twenty thousand. Especially popular were the gladiators. As in other Roman cities, the people of Corinth delighted in these bloody contests. They also were thrilled by an occasional novelty, as when condemned criminals were sent into the arena to fight wild animals. Corinth also had a roofed theater seating about three thousand. This cultural center dispensed the more refined arts of music and drama. The Corinthians no doubt had their favorite athletes and entertainers just as Americans do today.

Corinth had its religions. All the world religions were represented there. The ancient Greek gods and goddesses were still worshiped. Eastern mystery religions also were popular. The Egyptian religion of Isis was the favorite of many. The Jews had a synagogue there.

However, the most famous cult in Corinth was that of Aphrodite. In the old city of Corinth before its destruction by the Romans, the worship of Aphrodite flourished. Aphrodite was worshiped elsewhere in Greece, but her worship took a unique form in Corinth. Ancient sources say that a thousand prostitutes served in the temple of Aphrodite. This mixture of sexual immorality and religion was similar to the paganism encountered by Israel in Old Testament times—especially in the confrontation with Baal worship. In fact, the worship of Aphrodite in Corinth was probably an imported version of the Phoenician worship of Astarte. Astarte (called Astoreth or Ashtoreth in the Old Testament) was the female consort of Baal in the ancient fertility religion of the Canaanites.

This immoral worship of Aphrodite had brought wealth and fame—or infamy—to the old city of Corinth. This sort of religion blended well into the easy morality of a great seaport city. In an age noted for its sexual immorality, ancient Corinth gained a reputation as the most licentious city of its day. We cannot say for sure whether this same kind of worship still flourished in Paul's day. Ancient sources are not clear at this point, and archaeology has not yet been able to provide a sure answer. The temple with its official prostitutes may not have been there in Paul's day, but the cult probably still flourished in local shrines and around the docks. Paul's letter reveals that sexual immorality was still very much a part of the life of first-century Corinth.

This was the kind of city Paul entered when he arrived in Corinth. It was the kind of city in which he preached the gospel and organized a church. It was the kind of city in which the believers lived to whom Paul wrote his letters.

Corinth was not a modern metropolis of our technological age. Corinth obviously did not have some of our more complex urban problems. On the other hand, Corinth had those marks of urban culture that are true of cities of every age—including our own. Basically, these are the problems of a very large number of people living very close together. We have seen in this description of Corinth many of the traits of most modern cities—commerce, industry, political life, entertainment. Corinth was a melting pot of many kinds of people in a cosmopolitan setting that spawned social, economic, and moral problems of all kinds.

Getting Along Without God?

Does modern man need the gospel? Some people are quick to claim that modern man has outgrown his need for God, at least in the biblical sense. Modern man lives in a secular society where science, not religion, offers to solve his problems. Thus for many a modern city dweller, faith in God seems both impossible and unnecessary. Man who has now come of age no longer needs such false props as salvation, prayer, and divine strength.

This is the claim of one modern school of thought. And some facts seem to support their case. Whatever else may be said of the short-lived "death-of-God" movement in the sixties, many people do live their lives as if God were dead. Church attendance is on the decline. An increasing number of people believe that religion is losing its influence in American life. The churches and institutional religion in general are attacked as irrelevant and hypocritical—enemies of progress.

"See how well we are getting along without God." This is the boast of the self-confident humanists of today. George Buttrick is one who does not agree: "How can anyone intelligently say that modern man has outgrown his need for God? Or ever proclaim that we are 'Getting along very well' without God? Our industry lives with a gaping lesion: the strife between labor and capital. Our politics breeds wars that may destroy the whole world. Our culture is a hideous contrast between slums and suburbs, and between race and race. Violence makes our streets unsafe and nervous ills multiply. 'Getting along' is precisely what we are doing: we are falling apart—for lack of a creative faith."[4]

On an individual level, James Angell gives this insight into the need of America's modern city dwellers:

Man is crowded, but lonely.
He is rich, but poor.
He is busy, but bored.
He is surrounded by thirty-five institutions dedicated to his security . . . yet he is afraid, afraid even of the man across the street.
He has everything to do, yet nothing that really seems to matter in the long run.
He ignores religion, but is starved for God.[5]

Urban mission strategy. In these respects, the modern urbanite is little different from the residents of Corinth in the middle of the first century. About that time a lone Jewish traveler entered Corinth. This was not unusual, for many travelers—including Jews—passed through the city. But Paul had come to preach the gospel to the urbane Corinthians.

The account of Paul's work in Corinth is found in Acts 18:1–18. In reading through this part of the book of Acts, it is apparent that Paul's strategy was to concentrate his missionary efforts on the great urban centers. He came to Corinth from the key cultural city of Athens. Paul spent over eighteen months in Corinth. His next major campaign was in the city of Ephesus. Paul spent over two years in that strategic urban area (see Acts 19:8–10). Paul also was determined to go to Rome, the hub of the entire Empire. The book of Acts closes with the apostle in the capital of the Empire.

As we have already noted, the result of this strategy was that the key churches of the New Testament were city churches. Paul's longest and most important letters were those written to the churches in these cities. Those who arranged the letters of Paul in their present order were guided more by length and importance than by the order in which Paul actually wrote the letters. Thus it is no accident that Romans and the Corinthian letters stand first.

Thus in a sense, William Baird is right when he says that Paul helped "to change Christianity from a rural to an urban faith."[6] The history of cities goes back to the earliest days of history. A city is mentioned as early in the Old Testament as Genesis 4:17, but the primary setting of the Old Testament was rural. The same is true of the Gospels. The city of Jerusalem played a key role in the story of Jesus, but most of his ministry was centered in the rural countryside and small towns. As Baird observes, "Jesus saw people as sheep without a shepherd; Paul saw them as athletes ready to run a race."[7]

As Christianity moved outside the land of its birth, it entered an increasingly urban culture. As Paul followed the leadership of the Lord's Spirit, he realized that only an urban strategy could reach the Greco-Roman world. This helps us answer the question, Why did Paul concentrate on the cities? And this in turn helps answer the even more important question, Why must we Christians today concentrate our efforts on the cities?

Cities were where the people were in Paul's day. Cities are where the people are today. This does not mean that people in rural areas are unimportant. But Paul saw that if the cities were reached, the message could spread beyond to the country. The final result of Paul's work in Ephesus, for example, was that the gospel spread from this urban center throughout the entire province of Asia (see Acts 19:10). In the same way, the gospel spread throughout the province of Achaia from Corinth. Paul's second letter to Corinth was addressed not only to "the church of God which is at Corinth" but also to "all the saints who are in the whole of Achaia" (2 Cor. 1:1). There was a church, for example, in Cenchreae, a nearby suburb of Corinth (see Rom. 16:1). Thus on the basis of Paul's experience, we may state a general conclusion: A missionary strategy that places priority on the cities has the best possibility of reaching the most people in the city and in the country.

Christian witness in a secular age. The book of Acts reveals Paul's missionary strategy for work within the cities. He consistently followed two principles: (1) He went first to those who had been best prepared to respond positively to the gospel. (2) He also launched out boldly to witness to the untouched pagans wherever he could find them.

Paul began his work in Corinth by going to the synagogue each sabbath day. There he engaged both Jews and God-fearing Gentiles in conversation. The Jews, of course, had been providentially prepared to receive the Messiah. The God-fearing Gentiles shared the Jewish faith in one God and in his way set forth in the Scriptures. Thus Paul had a common heritage with these people. He could begin his witness with the sacred Scriptures, which all of them revered. He could point to Jesus as the Messiah promised in the Old Testament. Titius Justus was one of the God-fearing Gentiles who was converted under Paul's guidance. Crispus, the synagogue leader, was among the Jews converted (see Acts 18:7).

But Paul did not restrict his efforts to Jews and God-fearers. He also sought those who had no knowledge of the Jewish religion or the Old Testament. The Philippian jailer described in Acts 16:23–34 is a good example of such a person. He was among the kinds of persons Paul sought to win. Paul's strategy was to go outside the synagogue to seek such people. In Athens he witnessed in the market-place and in the hearing room (see Acts 17:16–34). In Ephesus, Paul rented a lecture hall in the middle of the city (see Acts 19:8–9). There he met the people of Ephesus on their own ground. And many responded.

We have both kinds of people today. One group has a Christian heritage. Their background and training has conditioned them to have a certain reverence for the Bible. They believe in God, Christ, the church and many other Christian teachings. Some of these people have been raised in Christian homes. Others have merely grown up in a part of the country where these teachings are accepted parts of the culture. But many of these people are not Christians. They believe the Bible, but they do not follow its teachings. Often they do not even know much of what it says. They believe about God and Christ, but they have made no personal commitment of faith. They give lip service to Christian standards of morality, but they do not practice them. They speak respectfully of churches, but they seldom attend church.

In spite of these factors, however, these people do have some preparation for responding to the gospel. They are comparable to the Jews and God-fearers of Paul's day. They can be appealed to on the basis of the authority of the Bible. They have some awareness of their sin and of their need for salvation in Christ.

Another segment of our society has no such background. They are strictly children of the secular age. They have been raised in homes where church attendance was not even a live option. They have been educated to believe that the Bible is an out-dated and irrelevant record of ancient history. They are only vaguely aware of Christian beliefs about God and Christ—names they know best as swear words. Some are actual atheists; all are "practical atheists," who live as if there were no God.

A father and his son stood looking up into the night sky at the twinkling stars. The boy surprised his father by asking, "How many of them did we put up there, Dad?" Only a secular child of the space age would ask this. A child with a different heritage would have a sense of awe and reverence at God's vast universe. This boy—so typical of many in our day—thought only of the few trinkets that man has thrust up into the sky.

Where do we begin to try to reach this secular generation with the gospel? It is encouraging to realize that Paul faced a somewhat comparable situation in trying to witness to the pagans of his day. Paul's description of the untouched Gentiles of his day also fits the modern secular generation. They are "separated from Christ, . . . strangers to the covenants of promise, having no hope and without God in the world" (Eph. 2:12).

Leander Keck in his book on Acts, *Mandate to Witness,* says that modern Christian witnesses are closer to the situation in Acts than believers have been for sixteen hundred years. Then as now Christians faced the frontier situation of a world without Christendom. Keck believes that the modern spirit of secularism and humanism makes this generation post-Christian in its outlook and actions: "This is not an anti-religious, anti-God movement because it does not regard religion or God as worth fighting any longer. In fact, this view simply bypasses God altogether and regards the whole idea of religion as being as outdated as a hitching-post."[8]

Paul faced this challenge armed only with his witness for Christ. At times, he was almost overwhelmed by the task. After a discouraging response in Athens, Paul came to Corinth. The situation was both challenging and frightening. The people were so many, and the needs were so great. God spoke to Paul: " 'Do not be afraid, but speak and do not be silent; for I am with you, and . . . I have many people in this city' " (Acts 18:9–10). Thus encouraged, Paul launched his mission to the city of Corinth.

Problems of a City Church

Seldom has the gospel been planted in more unyielding soil than in Corinth. The power of the gospel resulted in conversions. And a fledgling church was started. But the difficulties faced in living for Christ in a pagan city had only begun. The seed had been sown; the plants had begun to grow; but the weeds were ready to stunt their growth and to choke out their fruitfulness.

Paul was aware of this, and he was anxious to do whatever he could to help and encourage the new converts at Corinth. Paul was an evangelist, but he also was a teacher. His missionary strategy laid stress not only on reaching people but also on nurturing them in Christian growth. On the one hand, no one was more zealous to reach the unreached with the gospel. The distant horizons drew Paul like a magnet. He wanted to cross the mountains and seas in order to tell men the good news of Christ. On the other hand, no one was more committed to the practice of Christian teaching and training than Paul was. Wherever he preached, he tried to organize churches and to help new converts begin to grow in faith.

The book of Acts makes this clear. Paul spent a year in Antioch, teaching the people (see Acts 11:26). On his first missionary journey, he was driven out of Iconium. In Lystra he was stoned. Yet as he returned on his homeward journey, he revisited these cities. He did this in order to strengthen and encourage the converts in these cities (see Acts 14:21–22).

Paul's letters also make this principle of missionary strategy perfectly clear. These letters were not evangelistic tracts written to non-Christians. They were letters written to churches and individual Christians, instructing them and challenging them to be true to Christ. In God's plan, these letters became part of the New Testament. As a result, later generations of believers are instructed and inspired by them. The degree of Paul's continuing interest in the Corinthian Christians can be measured by the two letters to the church at Corinth. These two letters constitute by far the longest of Paul's extant correspondence with any church.

From scattered references we can reconstruct some of the things that happened in Corinth after Paul left. This, in turn, should help explain why Paul wrote 1 Corinthians.

Internal tensions. After Paul left Corinth, Apollos went there. Prior to that time, Apollos had come to Ephesus from Alexandria. He was an eloquent speaker, well-versed in the Old Testament. However he had not been instructed in all aspects of God's revelation in Christ. Paul's friends Aquila and Priscilla helped Apollos in this regard. So when Apollos went to Corinth, he went with his eloquent powers and a full knowledge of the Christian way. His ministry in Corinth proved to be helpful. Not only did he help the believers but he also continued Paul's strategy of bold proclamation of Christ to unbelievers (see Acts 18:24–28).

Meanwhile, Paul arrived in Ephesus to begin his lengthy ministry in that great city across the Aegean Sea from Corinth. Since leaving Corinth, Paul had been to Caesarea, Jerusalem, and Antioch. He also had visited the churches of Galatia and Phrygia. When he arrived in Ephesus, Apollos was still in Corinth (see Acts 19:1). Toward the end of his ministry in Ephesus, Paul wrote 1 Corinthians (see 1 Cor. 16:8–9). By that time, Apollos had left Corinth and had come to Ephesus (see 1 Cor. 16:12). No doubt, Apollos brought Paul up to date on what was happening in Corinth.

Apollos and Paul were friends and fellow workers, but some contrasts were apparent in their style of ministry.

Apollos was an eloquent speaker whose preaching was more appealing to some people than Paul's was. Some of the Corinthians could not help but compare and contrast these two men who had served in their midst. Some stated a strong preference for Apollos' style of ministry; others were equally insistent that Paul's way was better.

Peter may have visited Corinth at some time in this period. We have no record of such a visit, but we do know that some of the Corinthians preferred Peter to either Paul or Apollos (see 1 Cor. 1:12). Peter himself may not have been in Corinth, but the Corinthians were aware of his work and of his distinctively Jewish approach to Christianity. Therefore, some of the Corinthian believers—perhaps the Jews among them—stated a strong preference for Peter's approach to the gospel.

At some time in this period, Paul wrote a letter to Corinth. This letter was written prior to the letter called 1 Corinthians in the New Testament. Paul referred to this letter in 1 Corinthians 5:9. This early letter dealt with the problem of relationships with sinful and immoral people. This reflects what continued to be a crucial problem in the immoral city of Corinth. Paul had urged believers to avoid entangling relations with such people. The apostle was particularly concerned about church members who were continuing to live by pagan, non-Christian standards. He advocated that genuine believers disassociate themselves from such people (see 1 Cor. 5:10–11).

Troubling questions. The Corinthians responded to Paul's letter with a letter of their own. In this letter they raised some of the questions that were troubling them. The structure of 1 Corinthians gives us the clue to what these questions were. First Corinthians 7:1 begins, "Now concerning the matters about which you wrote." Then Paul proceeded to discuss Christian marriage. A similar formula is found in 1 Corinthians 8:1, "Now concerning food offered to idols." This formula is found again in reference to spiritual gifts (12:1) and to the financial collection for the saints (16:1). These were questions that troubled the Corinthian Christians; therefore they asked Paul to help answer the questions.

The letter from Corinth was probably carried to Paul by the three men mentioned in 1 Corinthians 16:15–18. Stephanus and his household were the first converts of Paul in Achaia. He had continued to be a devoted Christian worker in the Corinthian church. He along with Fortunatus and Achiacus had come from Corinth to visit Paul in Ephesus. Paul was a warm friend of these men. Even if they did bring the letter from Corinth, they no doubt also brought Paul more detailed information about the situation there.

In that age of travel, Paul talked to other people who came to Ephesus from Corinth. He mentions one such group in 1 Corinthians 1:11: "It has been reported to me *by Chloe's people* that there is quarreling among you, my brethren". These people may have been members of Chloe's family, but they probably were her slaves. Chloe was apparently someone known at least by name to the Corinthians. But we do not know whether or not she was a Christian, or whether she lived at Ephesus, Corinth, or somewhere else. We do know that some of those attached to her household had been to Corinth. When they came to Ephesus, they told Paul what they observed in the Corinthian church. They themselves were probably Christians.

So Paul had two kinds of sources of information about the situation in Corinth. Their letter raised certain specific questions. The oral reports spelled out other problems not mentioned in the letter. Paul learned, for example, about the dissension in the church. The Corinthians had divided up sides on the basis of their preference for a certain leader—Paul, Apollos, Cephas, Christ (see 1:12). Their basic lack of regard for one another was also apparent in other ways. Some of them were engaging in legal disputes with fellow church members (6:1). And their factious spirit was even being carried over into their worship services. They argued about wearing apparel and hairstyle (11:2–16). Even the Lord's Supper, which should have affirmed their oneness in Christ, had become an occasion for expressing their strife and discord (11:17–22).

Paul also found out that some of the Corinthians were questioning the basic Christian teaching of resurrection (15:12). As far as Paul was concerned, this kind of unbelief cut the very heart out of the Christian gospel and made Christian hope into a sham.

Cultural pressures. In addition to these problems, the Corinthians were struggling with the powerful influence of a sexually immoral culture. This was partially reflected in their question about marriage. But Paul learned of other things, such as a case of shocking immorality within the church itself. Paul was shocked that they not only tolerated this but actually condoned it (5:1). The whole moral climate of Corinth exerted a tremendous downward pull. Paul heard that some Corinthians were perverting salvation by grace into an excuse to disregard basic moral principles such as their attempt to justify sexual immorality because they were free from the law (6:12).

Scholars have tried to dig deeper into the evidence and determine if there was one main source of all the problems and questions in the Corinthian church. Some scholars believe that there was a group of Gnostics in Corinth. Gnosticism was a powerful force in the second century, and some scholars are convinced that it had begun as early as the time of Paul. The Gnostics undercut basic Christian beliefs and practices by their ideas and ways. And what was so insidious about this system was that the Gnostics professed to be especially spiritual and wise. They denied that material things could be good. Only soul or spirit is good; flesh and material things are evil. Based on this premise, they denied such basic doctrines as the incarnation (Christ only seemed to become flesh), the crucifixion (the human Jesus died, but not the divine Christ), and the resurrection (the soul is immortal, but the body cannot be restored to life). The Gnostic system of ethics tended either toward asceticism (the flesh is evil, so hold it in subjection) or toward libertinism (the flesh is evil, so it does not matter what a spiritual person does in his flesh).

You can see why some scholars believe that there were Gnostics in Corinth. The Corinthians were having the kinds of doctrinal and moral problems that are caused by gnosticism. On the one hand, they were minimizing the cross and denying the resurrection. On the other hand, they were proud of their own wisdom and spirituality. They prided themselves in their superior knowledge about meat sacrificed to idols, and in their superior spiritual gift of speaking in tongues. Some of them were refusing to marry (perhaps because it is fleshly), while others of them were indulging the flesh in sexual immorality.

All of these things are the kinds of things Gnostics would do. This has led some scholars to suggest that a gnostic party at Corinth was the main source of the problems there. However, more cautious scholars are content to say that there were some tendencies toward gnosticism in Corinth. Evidence is insufficient to assume a full-fledged gnostic party.

Actually, the situation at Corinth was probably much more complex than we can explain in terms of one factor. The closest we can come to a one-factor explanation is this:

The Corinthian believers were caught between the demands of their new faith and the pressures of their society. The Christian gospel consists of the unique message of God's redeeming love in Jesus Christ—particularly in his death and resurrection. This unique gospel was contrary to many of the currents of Greek thought and philosophy. Thus, the Corinthians were caught in the middle of this tension between the Christian faith and Greek thought.

Likewise, they were under strong pressures in their way of living. Many of the demands of Christianity were completely different from the accepted style of life in Corinth. This was true not only in the area of sensual sins. It was equally true in the area of priorities, personal relationships, and attitudes. According to the Corinthian style of life, a person was expected not only to surrender himself to every sensual pleasure but also to seize whatever he could claim for his own and to take pride in his superior attainments.

The believers in Corinth were *Christians,* but they also were *Corinthians.* Their problems and questions grew out of the tensions of trying to live for Christ in a non-Christian society. Often their problems, as Paul viewed them, were caused because the Corinthian Christians were not trying hard enough. Often they had allowed their culture, rather than their faith in Christ, to mold their ideas and life-style. The church was supposed to be a distinct community of faith, righteousness, and love in the midst of an unbelieving, ungodly, and unloving world. But the Corinthian church reflected the culture of Corinth more than it did the way of Christ.

Of course, this is the basic problem of believers in every generation, including our own. We too are caught between the pressures of society and the demands of Christ. Modern believers and churches are often more shaped by their culture than they are able to shape their culture. The currents of thought challenge the unique message and teachings of our faith. The moral and social climate of the age seeks to press us into a mold of conformity.

When Paul wrote 1 Corinthians, he was attempting to deal not only with the questions raised by the Corinthians in their letter but also with the deeper problems existing in the church—problems the Corinthians had not been willing to face. In 1 Corinthians, more than in any of his letters, Paul sought to apply Christianity to specific areas of life. In most of his letters, he devoted some space to practical application. But nearly all of 1 Corinthians is application.

This explains why 1 Corinthians is a book for today. Many of the questions raised by the Corinthians are questions asked by believers today. Many of the problems faced by the church at Corinth are reproduced in the twentieth century.

There are five large blocks of material in Paul's letter. Each of these sections deals with a different theme and area of application. Each of these areas of application is relevant for today. Each of the remaining chapters in this book will deal with one of these areas.

2 Man's Oldest Problem

The formal surrender of Japan at the end of World War II took place on the deck of the battleship Missouri in Tokyo Bay on September 2, 1945. As Supreme Allied Commander, General Douglas MacArthur signed the surrender document. His words on that occasion reveal a keen insight into the basic problem of human history and thus into the dilemma faced by modern man:

"Men since the beginning of time have sought peace. Various methods through the ages have attempted to devise an international process to prevent or settle disputes between nations. . . . Military alliances, balances of power, leagues of nations, all in turn failed, leaving the only path to be by way of the crucible of war. We have had our last chance. If we do not now devise some greater and more equitable system, Armageddon will be at our door. The problem basically is theological and involves a spiritual recrudescence and improvement of human character that will synchronize with our almost matchless advances in science, art, literature and all material and cultural developments of the past two thousand years. It must be of the spirit if we are to save the flesh."[1]

General MacArthur put his finger on our dilemma: our scientific and technological progress has far outstripped our progress in the art of living together as God intended. The worst war in human history had just been brought to an end. The long years of slaughter had been brought to an apocalyptic conclusion by the dropping of the atomic bombs on two hapless Japanese cities. The world marveled at the power unleashed by man's scientific know-how. And the world trembled at the prospect of man's misuse of this awesome new power. MacArthur was right: our moral and spiritual development desperately needs to match progress in other areas.

The record of human history does not offer much encouragement. Throughout history, men often have proved to be their own worst enemies. *Man's oldest problem has been himself.* Repeatedly, man has acted irrationally to his own hurt and ruin. He almost seems bent on his own destruction.

During the nineteenth century, many observers believed that man at long last had learned his lesson. Human progress was the order of the day—not only progress in science and technology but also some needed reforms in society itself. As a result, people were tempted to adopt an optimistic philosophy of inevitable human progress. Many expected the new twentieth century to usher in an era of unprecedented peace and progress.

But the easy optimism of the early years of the century was shattered by two world wars. Most of us began the second half of the century more firmly convinced than ever of the truth of the biblical doctrine of sin—man's fatal tendency to join in a rebellion against his own best interests.

Of course, the humanist is not completely wrong when he points to man's great potential. But the humanist's optimism is naive if he makes the mistake of painting a halo over every head. As God's unique creation, man has great potential for good; but man also has a fatal quirk at the core of his being. No serious effort to face our problems— individually or socially—can refuse to take note of this fact.

The first four chapters of Paul's letter to the Corinthians provide an ideal Bible base for examining man's oldest problem and for seeking ways to deal with the problem. Paul began by focusing on the main problem in the Corinthian church, which epitomizes the basic problem of human society (1:10–17).

Our Problem with Ourselves (1:10-17)

One of Abraham Lincoln's neighbors saw him lugging his two small sons down the street. Both boys—Willie and Tad—were bawling loudly. The neighbor asked, "Why Mr. Lincoln, what's the matter?" Lincoln answered: "Just what's the matter with the whole world. I've got three walnuts and each wants two."[2]

In the actions of his small sons, Lincoln saw mirrored the selfishness and strife that plagues the world. This small childhood episode thus reminded him of something much larger and far more serious.

In a similar way, the problem in the Corinthian church epitomizes for us the basic problem of humanity. The situation there is the basis for a study of the world's plight in miniature. The Corinthians themselves did not think that the situation was serious. Paul, however, considered it very serious, for they were acting just like the unredeemed people of the world.

Fighting in church. After a brief word of greeting, Paul launched a direct attack on the problem in the Corinthian church: "I appeal to you, brethren, by the name of our Lord Jesus Christ, that all of you agree and that there be no *dissensions* among you, but that you be united in the same mind and the same judgment. For it has been reported to me by Chloe's people that there is *quarreling* among you, my brethren" (1 Cor. 1:10–11).

The Greek word for "quarreling" *eris* is also found in 1 Corinthians 3:3, where Paul warned about "jealousy and *strife.*" The Greek sometimes used *eris* to refer to battles in a war. At other times they used the word to refer to political or domestic strife. Paul used the word here to refer to strife in the church—strife expressed in contention and quarreling. *Eris* describes the kind of wrangling that is a mark of sinful men. For example, in Galatians 5:20 Paul listed "strife" as one of the works of the flesh. And in Romans 1:29 he included this word as one of the sins that characterizes men who have turned their backs on God.

Paul spelled out what he meant by "dissensions" (v. 10) in verse 12: "What I mean is that each one of you says, 'I belong to Paul,' or 'I belong to Apollos,' or 'I belong to Cephas,' or 'I belong to Christ.' " The Corinthian believers were still together in one congregation. They had not divided into four separate groups. However, there was a spirit of dissension in the congregation because each individual had declared his loyalty to one leader.

Members of one faction boasted, "I belong to Paul." Among these were probably the church's charter members—those converted while Paul was there. They considered themselves loyal to Paul and his interpretation of the gospel.

A second group championed Apollos, whose ministry followed that of Paul. The members of this group probably had been impressed with Apollos' eloquence. They also liked his distinctive emphasis on wisdom.

Members of a third faction favored Cephas (the Aramaic name for Peter). Among this group were probably the Jewish members of the congregation. Perhaps they preferred a stronger emphasis on the old ways of the Jewish religion.

Much debate has been centered about the fourth party. Some interpreters say that there were only three parties; they explain the words "I belong to Christ" as spoken by those in Corinth who rejected an idolatrous attachment to any human leader. Other interpreters explain the words "I belong to Christ" as the battle cry of all the factions;

each was claiming that his faction—whether of Paul or Apollos or Cephas—was the true *Christian* party. However, most interpreters recognize the Christ-party as a fourth faction in Corinth. (The claims of all four groups are stated in parallel forms in verse 12, as if each was an actual faction in the church.)

If so, what did the members of this group claim? Various guesses have been made. Many modern scholars identify the Christ-party as Gnostics. According to this theory, these Gnostics professed a superior wisdom, a deeper spirituality, and a more profound knowledge of Christ than others possessed. It was as if they said, "I belong to Christ in a way that you do not belong to him."

As far as Paul was concerned, the real problem in Corinth was not the *beliefs* of these various factions; the real problem was the *existence* of the factions. In the Galatian letter Paul attacked the false teachings of those who had upset the churches of Galatia. However, in 1 Corinthians Paul did not attack false teachings; instead he attacked a false spirit of dissension and strife.

Who baptized you? This approach by Paul is clearly seen in verses 13–17. Paul chided the members of the Paul-faction in the church. He asked: "Is Christ divided? Was Paul crucified for you? Or were you baptized in the name of Paul?" (1 Cor. 1:13). This shows that the problem was in spirit, not doctrine. Had the problem been doctrinal (Gnostic or otherwise), Paul would have directed his fire against the heretics, not against his own supporters.

Paul rebuked his followers for confusing Paul with Christ. This kind of loyalty to a human leader—Paul or anyone else—is idolatrous. This is the point of Paul's words in verses 14–17. Why was Paul glad that he had baptized only a few in Corinth? Why did he make such a point of saying that Christ sent him not to baptize but to preach the gospel? The apostle surely was not making light of baptism. Rather he was pointing out an important fact about baptism: baptism creates a unique relationship between the one baptized and Christ, not between the one baptized and the one who baptizes him.

The important thing was not who baptized the Corinthian Christians; the important thing was that all of them had been baptized *into Christ*. They all were committed to Christ as Lord, and they all were members of his body. Yet they were not acting as if this were true: their idolatrous attachment to human leaders diverted their loyalty from Christ, and their factions actually dismembered the body of Christ.

A less perceptive man might have been flattered by the professed loyalty of his supporters. Can you imagine some of Paul's friends writing him after he left Corinth: "We miss you and your excellent leadership. Things will never be the same here without you. The new preacher Apollos is a good speaker; but his sermons are superficial compared to your messages." And Apollos' supporters may have said to him: "We are surely glad you came. Paul was a good man to get our church started, but he never was much of a preacher. Your sermons are much more inspiring."

Church leaders—pastors and teachers—are only human. Such professed loyalty flatters some leaders. Some even encourage it. This is a real temptation in a free church tradition, for such churches are strongly leader-oriented. A pastor—his personality, preaching, leadership—often is the most crucial influence in the life and work of a church. Thus a popular pastor can become the object of idolatrous loyalty, with or without his encouragement.

Paul certainly did not encourage such a spirit in Corinth. (Nor did Apollos for that matter.) Paul was able to look behind the facade of professed loyalty. What he saw did not please him, for what he saw was the basic sin of mankind—selfish pride.

"The Great Sin." The big word in verse 12 is *egō,* the Greek word for *I.* The Greek construction emphasizes the word "I" in each case. It was as if a man said: "Look at me. *I* belong to Paul." The emphasis was on *I,* not on Paul. This self-assertive spirit was the cause of the dissension and strife. When this kind of selfishness is at work, any issue can become the storm center of strife. Take the issue in Corinth, for example: who I support is actually much less important than the fact that *I* support him. Once committed to a position, selfish pride demands that *I* remain adamant. My leader is bound to be the best; after all, don't *I* support him? In situations such as this, the merits of the issue are beside the point. No amount of evidence or argument can move me; I dare not give in or *I* will lose face.

C. S. Lewis calls selfish pride "the great sin." He says: "Pride leads to every other vice: it is the complete anti-God state of mind."[3] Lewis explains the difference between pride that is good and pride that is sinful: "Pleasure in being praised is not Pride. The child who is patted on the back for doing a lesson well, the woman whose beauty is praised by her lover, the saved soul to whom Christ says 'Well done,' are pleased and ought to be. For here the pleasure lies not in what you are but in the fact that you have pleased someone you wanted (and rightly wanted) to please. The trouble begins when you pass from thinking 'I have pleased him; all is well,' to thinking, 'What a fine person I must be to have done it.' "[4]

When this attitude creeps in, selfish pride begins its evil work. Such pride is sinful because it separates a man from God, from others, and from the best he can be. Lewis points out that pride is so deadly in human society because it is essentially competitive: "Pride gets no pleasure out of having something, only out of having more of it than the next man. We say that people are proud of being rich, or clever, or good-looking, but they are not. They are proud of being richer, or cleverer, or better-looking than others."[5]

Can you imagine how this worked in Corinth? Probably the Corinthians began by stating honest preferences for certain leaders. But then pride asserted itself: they began to argue about leaders, and probably even to disparage other leaders and those who supported them. Thus selfish pride turned a church into a hotbed of dissension and strife. As the rest of Paul's letter reveals, this sin poisoned every aspect of the life of the Corinthian church.

This same sin poisons every aspect of human society. The pervasive power of selfish pride is seen in the way that it exerted its evil influence even in the church. The spirit of the world had gotten into the church. The church was supposed to exert a redeeming influence on the world; actually the world was exerting a corrupting influence on the church. The church was acting no differently than any other social unit in Corinth. The strife in the church was of the same basic character as cutthroat tactics in business, backstabbing in politics, bickering in homes, even fights-to-the-death in the arena.

In some ways 1 Corinthians 1:10–12 parallels Romans 1:18–32. The Romans passage contains Paul's dark picture of sin in the pagan world of his day. (He probably wrote Romans while he was in Corinth.) Paul described how men turn from God to senseless idolatry. This results in all manner of immoral perversions and a frightening variety of destructive social evils. The latter list catalogs many kinds of human strife—of the same kind as that found in the Corinthian church. As we have already noted, Paul even used the same word for *strife* in both passages.

Some commentators point out that the factions in the

Corinthian church were consistent with the history of Greece. The fatal flaw of the ancient Greeks was their inability to work together. They wore themselves down by arguing and fighting one another. They usually quit fighting one another only long enough to join in opposing a common foe. On occasion, they were not above allying themselves with an alien foe in order to get back at one another.

All of this was true of ancient Greece, but it also has been true of all human history to one degree or another. It is as true today as it ever was—among nations and within nations on down to the smallest social unit, the family. Strife among nations keeps the world on the brink of war in a day when nuclear war could mean the end of civilization as we know it. Strife—social, economic, and racial—polarizes our land and threatens the very life of the republic. Selfish pride, dissension, and strife poison the life stream of communities, businesses, homes, and even churches.

Over against this way of human pride and strife, Paul set the way of God—seen in the cross (vv. 18–25) and in the lives of men saved by God's grace (vv. 26–31).

God's Way and Man's Way (1:18-31)

A crude drawing has been found in the ruins of ancient Rome; it was obviously intended as a caricature of the crucifixion of Jesus. The drawing shows a man's body hanging on a cross, but the body has the head of an ass. To the left of the cross is a figure of a young man with his hand raised as if he is worshiping the person being crucified. The inscription beneath the drawing reads, "Alexamenos worships his god."[6]

This crude drawing and inscription were found by archaeologists in what was once a room beneath the imperial palace of ancient Rome. Indications are that the room was used as a prison. This is only one of many scrawlings on the walls. Not much imagination is needed to reconstruct a possible explanation: A young man named Alexamenos had become a Christian. He was probably a servant in the imperial palace; perhaps he was even a prisoner. The young man's faith in the crucified Savior subjected him and his Lord to the mockery of those who had no sympathy for his worship of Christ.

This is a revealing commentary on what Paul wrote in 1 Corinthians 1:18–31. In these verses Paul focused attention on the cross and on those who have been saved by the cross. By worldly standards the cross and those who believe in the crucified Christ are weak and foolish, but by God's standards the cross represents God's power and wisdom. As Paul put it: "The word of the cross is folly to those who are perishing, but to us who are being saved it is the power of God" (1:18).

Stumbling at the cross. Paul further spelled this out in verses 22–24: "For Jews demand signs and Greeks seek wisdom, but we preach Christ crucified, a stumbling block to Jews and folly to Gentiles, but to those who are called, both Jews and Greeks, Christ the power of God and wisdom of God."

The cross was a stumbling block to the Jews because they wanted a mighty deliverer, not a suffering Savior. The four Gospels show how quickly many Jews would have followed Jesus if he had been their kind of messiah. They wanted to make Jesus their king if he would feed them and lead them to victory. They expected him to prove himself by spectacular signs; then they were willing to follow him.

But Jesus refused to meet their terms. He resisted the temptation to be a popular Messiah. Instead he spoke to his disciples about a way of rejection, suffering, and death.

He saw what the Jews did not see: they wanted him to over-come their enemies and to meet their needs, but Jesus saw their enemies and needs differently than they did. He had come to grapple with a stronger enemy than Roman might. He had come to meet deeper needs than the obvious ones. Jesus knew that brute force could not overcome such enemies and meet such needs. He accepted the way of sacrificial love as the only way of salvation.

For a time the cross was a stumbling block even to his closest followers. When Jesus first predicted his coming crucifixion, Peter rebuked him for saying such a thing. Although Jesus continued to speak of his role as that of the Suffering Servant, the disciples never really grasped what he meant. At the time of the crucifixion the disciples thought the cross was a hopeless defeat. The resurrection of Jesus forced them to take another look at the cross; then they began to grasp what Jesus had tried to tell them. Led by God's Spirit, they began to preach the good news of God's love in the cross.

Ignoring the cross. When the early Christians began to preach Christ to the Gentiles, they ran into another mis-understanding of the cross. The cross was a stumbling block to the Jews; but it was sheer foolishness to the Gen-tiles, especially to the worldly-wise Greeks: "This meant for the one that the crucified Christ was an insult and therefore to be denied; for the other, he was irrelevant and therefore to be ignored."[7]

Imagine how Paul's message of the crucified Christ sounded to the Greeks: Paul told them of an obscure Jewish carpenter-turned-teacher who died the death of a criminal convicted of a capital crime. And Paul claimed that this crucified criminal was the Son of God and the Savior of the world!

The Christian preaching of the cross was foolish to the

Greeks because they were seeking *wisdom*. Throughout this passage Paul laid stress on wisdom as a key aspect of Greek life and thought. Philosophy was always important to the Greeks. They placed priority on elaborate systems of thought and on sophisticated methods of arguing a point. Thus the proclamation of the cross offended the Greeks in two ways—in its method of presentation and in its contents.

Christian preaching offended them. They preferred an eloquent orator or a skilful debater to a straightforward preacher. Paul mentioned this aspect of wisdom in 1:17, and he came back to it in 2:1–5. But in 1:18–25 Paul was primarily concerned with the seeming foolishness of the *contents* of the Christian message—the cross itself.

In this passage Paul contrasted what he called "the wisdom of the world" with "the wisdom of God." The wisdom of the world was exemplified by the Greeks, but Paul's meaning goes beyond this one manifestation of worldly wisdom. In verse 20 Paul mentioned not only "the wise man" and "the debater"; he also mentioned "the scribe." The scribe was probably the professional Jewish scribe who placed such emphasis on the fine points of the law. Jewish legalism was as much a manifestation of worldly wisdom as was Greek philosophy. Both systems had one thing in common: they were centered in men, not in God. They were essentially egocentric systems where man's basic pride was allowed full expression.

This does not mean that "the wisdom of the world" is necessarily atheistic or anti-religious. To the contrary, the Jewish legalists claimed their system was the way to be justified before God, and the Greek philosophers were far from antireligious. In fact, Paul observed that the Greeks were "very religious" (Acts 17:22). Each system claimed to be a way to God or to the gods. In both cases, however, man was in control: either by his works or by his wisdom.

Paul denied that men can find God in this way: "For since, in the wisdom of God, the world did not know God through wisdom, it pleased God through the folly of what we preach to save those who believe" (1:21). The cross seems foolish to the wisdom of the world, but the wisdom of the world seems foolish to God. The cross stands in judgment over all ways of man-made salvation—whether by works or by wisdom.

Glorying in the cross. The cross represents a way of divine grace for man the sinner. This is devastating to human pride—religious pride and humanistic pride. Evidence of man's deeply ingrained pride is seen in his negative reaction to the cross. The ancient Greeks are long since dead, but the wisdom of the world is still very much alive—both in its religious and in its secular forms.

Long ago, Christianity accepted the cross as its symbol. In some segments of Christendom, crosses are worn as ornaments and churches are adorned with crosses. In nonliturgical circles, we sing much and talk much about the cross. But often the essential message of the cross seems to elude us. Human pride remains intact. Egotism, dissension, even strife are still very much with us, just as they were with the Corinthian church.

When we come to discuss 1 Corinthians 2–4, we will deal in more detail with this fact. Suffice it to say here that the cross must be a power in our lives—the means whereby God's grace not only forgives us but also shapes us according to the will of God. Many people are willing to be religious, so long as they can be religious on their own terms. In such a religion, man is the potter and God is the clay. This is the religious manifestation of the wisdom of the world. It is comparable to the sign-seeking Jews who stumbled at Jesus' announcement of the cross.

The wisdom of the world is also present today in its non-religious, humanistic form. Men worship themselves—their wisdom, wealth, and prestige. Judged by these standards, the cross is as weak and foolish as it was to the Greeks of Paul's day. God's grace and self-giving love are objects of ridicule to the self-sufficient, self-made men of the world. Yet from the biblical point of view, this worldly pride in purely human wisdom is the reason for the mess we are in, and the cross represents our only hope of salvation—as individuals and as a society.

During World War II the German Air Force carried out massive bombing attacks against English cities. Coventry was a favorite target. Many of the city's buildings were destroyed by bombs and fire. Among these was the famous Coventry cathedral. Since the war, the cathedral has been rebuilt. Charred timbers from the burned cathedral were used to make a cross. Beneath the cross were written the words of Jesus, "Father, Forgive." One day an official of the cathedral found a man kneeling before the cross in tears. When the official offered to be of help, the man explained: "I was in the German Air Force and flew over Coventry the night the cathedral was bombed. Ever since that night, my heart has been sad because of that experience. Today, as I knelt here at the altar and read the inscription, 'Father, Forgive,' something happened within me—I found release."[8]

The world knows many kinds of power—power that can accomplish many things. But man's wisdom and power could not do for that man's guilt and deep need what only the power of the cross could do. The cross is the power of God's grace unleashed in the world. Where the cross is truly preached and lived, it still exerts this kind of power.

"Come, Ye Sinners, Poor and Needy." In verses 26–31 Paul made his point in a slightly different way. He moved from the cross itself to those saved by the cross. Just as God shows his wisdom and power in the cross itself, so does he through those saved by his grace.

Paul wrote to the Corinthians: "For consider your call, brethren; not many of you were wise according to worldly standards, not many were powerful, not many were of noble birth; but God chose what is foolish in the world to shame the wise, God chose what is weak in the world to shame the strong" (1:26–27). This is one of the best pieces of evidence we have to show the kinds of people who made up the early churches.

A striking confirmation of this fact comes from one of the foes of the early Christians. Celsus was a severe critic of Christianity. He wrote these words about the Christians of his day:

"Their injunctions are like this. 'Let no one educated, no one wise, no one sensible draw near. For these abilities are thought by us to be evils. But as for anyone ignorant, anyone stupid, anyone uneducated, anyone who is a child, let him come boldly.' By the fact that they themselves admit that these people are worthy of their God, they show that they want and are able to convince only the foolish, dishonorable and stupid, and only slaves, women, and little children."[9]

Both Paul and Celsus agreed that Christians were from the lower classes, but they drew different conclusions from this fact: Celsus assumed that this proved how ridiculous Christianity is. By contrast, Paul pointed to this fact as proof that grace is the basis of man's acceptance by God. This, in turn, shows how utterly false are the world's standards of greatness. The very people who are wise, powerful, and noble by worldly standards often feel no need of God and his grace.

The composition of the early church was a parable of God's grace. No man—rich or poor, educated or uneducated, well known or unknown—can boast before God. All pride is ruled out: "He is the source of your life in Christ Jesus, whom God made our wisdom, our righteousness and sanctification and redemption; therefore as it is written, 'Let him who boasts, boast of the Lord'" (1:30–31).

Paul practiced what he preached. He refused to take personal credit either for his salvation or for his life of dedicated service. Rather he testified, "By the grace of God I am what I am" (1 Cor. 15:10). At times Paul pointed to his own life, even using it as an example for others to follow; but he always was careful to remind his readers of the real source of his new life. In defending his claim to be an apostle, Paul wrote "I worked harder than any of them [the other apostles]," but he quickly added, "though it was not I, but the grace of God which is with me" (1 Cor. 15:10).

This dependence on the grace of God did not rob Paul of his individuality; rather it enabled him to become himself as God intended him to be. So it does for us. When we are most controlled by God's grace and power, we are most free to become ourselves as God intended for us to be.

Toscanini, the famous conductor, was very exacting, almost tyrannical in rehearsals. Once he was rehearsing an orchestra for a performance of the *Ninth Symphony* of Beethoven. At last the time came for the concert performance. Some of the orchestra members expected a final scolding. Instead Toscanini stood silent before them; finally he spoke: "Who am I? Who is Toscanini: Who are you? I am nobody! You are nobody . . ." He paused. The orchestra and audience waited. Then the conductor's face lighted up as he added, "But Beethoven is everything— EVERYTHING!"[10] And that night the orchestra outdid themselves; they played Beethoven's *Ninth Symphony* as they had never played it before.

Spiritually Retarded Christians (2.1 to 3:4)

In the days when westerns were regular Saturday afternoon fare at the movies, a small boy was always filled with questions as a movie began: "Who's the bad man? Who's the good guy?" This line of questioning continued until the hero and the villain were clearly identified. Then the little fellow leaned back and relaxed, usually even to the point of falling fast asleep.

Unfortunately in real life the bad guys and the good guys are not always so easy to identify. The distinctions are not always so clear cut. Ideally, the lives of Christian people should be distinctly different from the lives of non-Christians. Actually, this difference is not always apparent. The life-style of many professing Christians is little different from the way of non-Christians. Paul implied as much in 1 Corinthians 1:10–31; then in 2:1 to 3:4 he spelled it out clearly.

In this block of Scripture verses, Paul continued his contrast between the wisdom of the world and the wisdom of God. He had already mentioned that the Greeks stumbled at the *method* as well as the content of Christian preaching (see 1:17). The Greeks put great stock in eloquence and in a speaker's ability to use involved arguments to support elaborate theories. By contrast, Paul came to Corinth and preached "Jesus Christ and him crucified" (2:2). Paul reminded the Corinthians: "My speech and my message were not in plausible words of wisdom, but in demonstration of the Spirit and power" (2:4).

Spiritual and unspiritual men. In subsequent verses Paul picked up the mention of *the Spirit* and focused attention on the Spirit's role in helping men respond to God's revealed wisdom. Paul explained that Christians have a wisdom of their own that is different from the world's wisdom. This "secret and hidden wisdom of God" (2:7) is not understood by worldly-wise men, but the truly mature are enabled to grasp this wisdom because the Spirit reveals it to them.

Paul's terminology in verses 6–13 is similar to that of the mystery religions of his day. He used their words—*a secret and hidden wisdom imparted to the mature*. The mystery religions claimed a special insight into the mysteries for those initiated into the secrets of their religion. At first glance Paul seems to be making the same point; but Paul was actually saying something very different. He was not teaching that Christianity offers a special wisdom to the spiritually initiated inner circle. The only mystery Christ offers is the revealed wisdom of God's grace, and this mystery is offered to all men. The Spirit seeks to reveal God's grace to all men, but some men refuse to listen. They tune out God's Spirit. They consider God's wisdom to be weak and foolish. Since God's wisdom cannot be discovered by men in their own ways and controlled by men on their own terms, they will have none of it.

In verses 14–16 Paul contrasted the unspiritual man and the spiritual man. The "spiritual" man of verse 15 is only another name for the "mature man" of verse 6. He is not naturally endowed with special spiritual insight. Rather he is a recipient of God's grace imparted by God's Spirit. Thus he does not boast of his own spirituality; instead he praises God for divine grace. The difference between him and the unspiritual man is that he is open to the Spirit's revelation and work in him.

The unspiritual man is not under the control of God's Spirit because he has not chosen to be led by the Spirit. He is a man of the world whose values and standards are physical and material, not moral and spiritual. He values what he can see and feel and count; unseen moral and spiritual values do not seem important to him. "The unspiritual man does not receive the gifts of the Spirit of God, for they are folly to him" (2:14).

Several years ago, John Foster Dulles gave an address at Princeton University. He spoke of the need to bring spiritual attitudes to bear on political problems. He referred several times in his speech to "the Holy Spirit." Afterwards, a man of irreligious temper asked a friend: "What does Dulles mean by 'the Spirit'? What does he mean?"[11] Commenting on this kind of person, Paul W. Hoor says: "He is awkward before the world of the Spirit that surrounds us and that relates all else together. It is as if there is a language he cannot talk. There is a key he does not have. There is a system of calculation and measurement he cannot employ. It's like being in a foreign country and not being able to talk the language and hence not being able to enter into its life."[12]

Carnal Christians. Throughout chapter 2 Paul wrote in idealistic terms; that is, he wrote as if all Christians were mature men of the Spirit. However, the apostle dealt more realistically with the Corinthian situation in 3:1–4: "But I, brethren, could not address you as spiritual men, but as men of the flesh, as babes in Christ. I fed you with milk, not solid food; for you were not ready for it; and even yet you are not ready, for you are still of the flesh. For while there is jealousy and strife among you, are you not of the flesh, and behaving like ordinary men? For when one says, 'I belong to Paul,' and another, 'I belong to Apollos,' are you not merely men?"

The Corinthian believers were men who supposedly had been touched by God's Spirit; but their actions were like the unspiritual, not the spiritual. Paul referred to them as "brethren," and he acknowledged that they were "in Christ"; but he charged that they were acting like "men of the flesh." Paul often used the term *flesh* to refer to men living apart from God's Spirit. A man of the flesh is the same thing as an unspiritual man. Paul did not charge that the Corinthian believers were men of the flesh untouched by the Spirit, but he did charge that they were acting like unspiritual men.

In the first century the problem of spiritual immaturity was not confined to the Corinthian church. The writer of Hebrews addressed his readers in words almost parallel to Paul's words in 1 Corinthians 3:1–4 (see Heb. 5:11–14). And this problem was not confined to churches of the first century. Spiritual immaturity of Christians continues to be a problem that paralyzes the churches' effectiveness—perhaps the greatest internal problem faced by modern churches.

C. R. Daley, Jr., wrote these penetrating words about spiritual retardation among Baptists: "Spiritual retardation is one of the chief explanations for so many Baptist dropouts, and is the source of so much dissension and trouble in the churches. Not all the spiritual babies drop out. Some stay in the church, and act like the babies they are. There is some similarity between mental and spiritual retardation. Like mental retardation, spiritual retardation affects different people differently. Some mentally retarded persons are violent and dangerous. They have the physical strength of a man and the mind of a baby. The same is true of some spiritually retarded. They lash out at each other like babies; they try to destroy the pastor or anyone else who gets in their way. Other spiritually retarded are quiet, gentle, and even sweet-spirited like some mentally retarded. They are easy to love and give no trouble. However, they require constant attention as do babies and they make no productive contribution."[13]

How can this be? How can believers in Christ continue to act more like men of the flesh than men of the Spirit? Part of the blame is a superficial view of what is meant by being a Christian. By one definition, being a Christian means quitting your worldly pleasures and joining the church. This view overlooks the New Testament definition of *sins of the flesh*. According to the popular view, the sins of the flesh refer only to outward and obvious sins—like drunkenness and immoral living. Of course, some professing Christians have not even given up these kinds of sins (see 1 Cor. 5–6); but others have merely exchanged one fleshly sin for another. They have given up the outward and obvious sins of the flesh, but they have not given up the selfish pride that is at the heart of all sin. Paul's list of the "works of the flesh" includes not only such obvious evils as "drunkenness and carousing" but also such less obvious sins as "strife, jealousy, anger, selfishness, dissension, party spirit, envy" (Gal. 5:19–21). These latter sins of attitude, disposition, and interpersonal relations are at the heart of the worldly way of life. A church that is dominated by such sins is no different in actions than any social unit of the world. A Christian who practices such sins is guilty of worldliness.

Conversion: beginning or end? Again we ask: How can this be? How can Christians act in this way? Unfortunately, many Christians mistake the *beginning* of the Christian life for the *end*. They make a profession of faith; then they sigh and say, "I'm glad *that's over!*" What they fail to realize is that it is not over; it has only *just begun!*

A distortion of our evangelical tradition may be partly to blame for this. The importance of conversion cannot be overemphasized, but neither can the importance of Christian growth.

Shortly after World War II, Dr. Ellis Fuller was invited to speak on a nationwide radio program. The network required the preacher to submit a manuscript of his sermon prior to delivery. A network official called Dr. Fuller and asked that one word be deleted from his sermon. Dr. Fuller wanted to say something about the world's future hopes for peace. He had written: "I hope every person who sits around the peace table will be a Christian." The network official asked him to take out the word *a*. Then the sentence would read: "I hope every person who sits around the peace table will be Christian."[14] Dr. Fuller carefully explained to the official how completely this would change his meaning. Being Christian is not the same as being *a* Christian. A non-Christian can be Christian in many areas of his life-style, but he needs to become a Christian if he is to be Christian at the deepest level of life.

This is a clear New Testament teaching. Many evangelical churches have been faithful in proclaiming this truth, but they have slighted an equally clear New Testament teaching in failing to give emphasis to the importance of continued Christian growth. A man needs to become a Christian before he can grow as a Christian; but when he does become a Christian, he should begin to grow as a Christian.

How is this to be done? Not by sheer human effort. This would become only a system of human works that still subtly feeds the appetite of human pride. Paul's emphasis was on the continuing work of God's grace in our lives by his Spirit. The Spirit of God does not complete his work in us at conversion; to the contrary, he only begins his work. Christian growth takes place when a believer continues to lay his life as open to God's Spirit as he did when he first was saved. The fruit of the Spirit is not man-made; it is wrought by God. A Christian's part is to cultivate the soil of his heart so that God can grow such qualities in his life.

Living Outside Ourselves (3:5 to 4:21)

Throughout the first four chapters of 1 Corinthians, Paul continued to address himself to the problem of dissension. However, toward the end of his attack on this problem, he said something that may seem to undermine his whole argument. He wrote, "I urge you, . . . be imitators of me" (4:16). In the larger context of this statement, Paul wrote about the service, stewardship, and sacrifices of himself and the other apostles. He had been warning against pride and egotism. At first sight, his challenge to follow his example may seem to be a case of pride on Paul's part. Perhaps his enemies in Corinth even accused him of bragging. But this was not Paul's intention.

Paul was speaking as a father does to his children. He considered himself as more than a teacher and guide to the Corinthian Christians; he thought of himself as their "father in Christ Jesus through the gospel" (4:15). Small children learn by imitating their parents—how they talk, how they walk, how they act. To paraphrase what Paul was saying to the Corinthians: "Watch how I do it. Learn from me and the other apostles. Here is the way you should be living: Our loyal *service*, faithful *stewardship*, and unselfish *sacrifice* provide a pattern for you."

Not to be served but to serve. *Service* is one of the key concepts in 1 Corinthians 3:5-23. After rebuking the Corinthians for their idolatrous loyalty to himself and Apollos, Paul wrote: "What then is Apollos? What is Paul? Servants through whom you believed, as the Lord assigned to each.

I planted, Apollos watered, but God gave the growth. So neither he who plants nor he who waters is anything, but only God who gives the growth" (3:5-7).

Paul pictured himself and Apollos as fellow workers, laboring in the same field—Corinth. Each worked in the field according to his own abilities, and each was completely dependent on God for causing life and growth.

Then Paul changed the analogy; instead of working in a field, he and Apollos were constructing a building—the temple of God, the church. In this building, Paul laid the foundation—the only possible foundation for the temple of God: "For no other foundation can anyone lay than that which is laid, which is Jesus Christ" (3:11). Those who work in and through the church build on this foundation. Some, like Apollos, build a beautiful and lasting structure. Others build in a less worthy fashion, their structures proving unable to stand the tests of time and eternity.

The main point in verses 5-23 is the folly of idolizing human leaders. Leaders are worthy of respect and loyalty, but not the kind of idolatrous attitude shown in Corinth. Paul and Apollos were only servants of God. Every true Christian leader is at best a servant of God. Thus how foolish for anyone—leader or people—to forget this and to put a leader in the place of God. Here are Paul's words: "So let no one boast of men. For all things are yours, whether Paul or Apollos or Cephas or the world or life or death or the present or the future, all are yours; and you are Christ's; and Christ is God's" (3.21-23).

This passage raises a crucial question about the church: Whose is the church? To whom does the church belong? Does the church belong to the leaders? the members? the Lord? Paul's answer is that the church belongs ultimately to the Lord. Even the apostles were only servants of the Lord. Christ is the foundation of the church. The church is brought into being by the Lord, and it is sustained by him. Thus, in this ultimate sense, the church belongs not to the pastor, nor to the deacons, nor to the members, but to the Lord.

On the other hand, there is a sense in which the church belongs to those who are the church. The church is the people of God. As God's people, we belong not only to the Lord but also to one another. In this relationship of mutual interdependence, church members need not only the Lord but also one another. Paul dealt with this in more detail later in his letter (see 1 Cor. 12), but he laid the foundation here.

Throughout this passage, Paul was emphasizing the apostles' example of service. The Corinthians were quarreling about places of prominence and greatness. By contrast, the apostles were practicing that kind of greatness taught by the Lord, who measures greatness in terms of service. Paul was using their example of service to challenge the Corinthians as he did the Galatians, "Through love be servants of one another" (Gal. 5:13).

What is expected of a trustee? Paul began chapter 4 by referring once again to himself and the other apostles as servants, but he added another word also—the word *stewards*. A steward is a trustee. As God's stewards, the apostles had been entrusted with the revealed mysteries of God's grace. The test by which stewards are judged is faithfulness: A good steward faithfully discharges his trust; he uses what God has entrusted to him in the way God expects him to use it.

The basic idea in stewardship is responsibility, but 1 Corinthians 4:1–7 does not present faithful stewardship as a heavy burden to be borne. Actually, Paul's sense of ultimate responsibility to Christ had a liberating effect on his life. Paul's one goal was to please the Lord; therefore he was neither flattered nor tyrannized by what others said about him. This set him free to be the man God intended for him to be. Had Paul made status or popularity his goal, these tyrants would have given him no peace; but Paul was free under Christ's yoke.

Paul saw his stewardship as a gift as well as a demand. For Paul, everything in the Christian life is a gift of God. God never demands what he does not, first of all, give—and far more. Because of this, no Christian can take selfish pride in God's gifts, precisely because they are gifts. Paul clearly spelled this out for the Corinthians: "I have applied all this to myself and Apollos for your benefit, brethren, that you may learn by us to live according to scripture, that none of you may be puffed up in favor of one against another. For who sees anything different in you? *What have you that you did not receive?* If then you received it, why do you boast as if it were not a gift?" (1 Cor. 4:6–7).

A picnic or a crusade? Paul then pressed home his point in a series of vivid contrasts between the high and lofty Corinthians and the battered and bruised apostles (see 4:8–13). *Sacrifice* is the key idea in these verses. The Corinthians acted as if being a Christian meant ruling like a king. Yet by contrast the apostles were like condemned men facing death in the arena. Paul continued the series of contrasts in these words: "We are fools for Christ's sake, but you are wise in Christ. We are weak, but you are strong. You are held in honor, but we in disrepute. To the present hour we hunger and thirst, we are ill-clad and buffeted and homeless, and we labor working with our own hands. When reviled, we bless; when persecuted, we endure; when slandered, we try to conciliate" (4:10–13).

Paul was not trying to impress the Corinthians with what he and the other apostles had done. He was trying to remind them of what is involved in following Christ—a cross-bearing, self-denying way of life. He was illustrating by example what he had written earlier about the wisdom of God in the cross of Christ. This is the wisdom of the cross—a life of self-giving love. "Discipleship is not a life of a king, but a life of a servant, not a life of self-esteem, but a life of self-giving."[15]

Paul obviously considered the cross as more than the entrance to the Christian life; the cross is also the pattern by which the Christian life is to be lived. This does not mean that Paul defined being a Christian as trying to follow Jesus' example of self-giving love. This would imply that a man could do this in his own strength. Instead, Paul spoke of sharing the cross-resurrection experience of Christ because the Spirit of the crucified-risen Lord controlled his life. The cross and resurrection were historical events, but they are more than historical events—they are part of a Christian's present experience. The cross-resurrection life in Christ is the *pattern* of self-giving and the *power* to live such a life. Paul exemplified what this means in actual experience. The same should be true of every believer.

John Henry Jowett once observed that a true Christian experience of the cross changes life "from a picnic into a crusade."[16] A picnic is a time for personal relaxation and pleasure. A crusade calls for work, dedication, and sacrifice. Many modern Christians, like the ancient Corinthians, approach life as if it were a picnic. That is, they are concerned for themselves—their own comfort and convenience. Their church life, homelife, business life, social life are all basically self-centered. They are looking for what they can draw from life, not for what they can give to life. The cross is not a principle of daily life for them.

Gerald Kennedy tells of a motel near the famous shrine at Lourdes, France. The motel is called "Gethsemane," an appropriate title for a motel near a religious shrine. Like many motels the Gethsemane motel has a sign reading "with all modern comforts."[17] This is a parable on the religion of many people. We want a religion with Gethsemane and Calvary for Jesus, but we want our own experience to include all the comforts and conveniences of a self-centered life.

A group of children had been memorizing Bible verses in Vacation Bible School. Each child was to recite one verse at the commencement service. One small boy had memorized John 14:18. He had practiced until he could say it perfectly: "I will not leave you comfortless: I will come to you." However, when his time came to say his verse, his nervousness caused him to give a different version. He quoted Jesus as saying, "I will not leave you *comfortable:* I will come to you."[18] This unintentional mistake states a truth as great as the correct version: The Lord's Spirit is the great Comforter when we are afflicted, troubled, or bereaved; but he is the great Convicter when we are sinful, complacent, or indifferent. Paul was following the Spirit's direction in trying to shatter the complacency of the Corinthian Christians. He was trying to challenge them to live by the way of the cross rather than by the way of selfish pride. Because their sins are our sins also, we cannot afford to turn a deaf ear to Paul's plea.

Paul did not end this plea in chapter 4. Although he did not use the same words to describe it, he continued his plea throughout his letter. Instead of the wisdom of God in the cross, Paul spoke of Christian love, using the Greek word *agapē* for the kind of love he had in mind. The hymn of Christian love in 1 Corinthians 13 is among the most famous parts of the letter, but the *agapē* of chapter 13 is only another way of describing the way of the cross set forth at the beginning of the letter. This is the ultimate Christian answer to man's oldest problem of selfish pride and the strife that goes with it.

The following prayer of Francis of Assisi exemplifies Christian *agapē*. Imagine what would happen if Christians prayed and lived by this principle of the cross. What a difference in churches . . . homes . . . communities . . . the world!

"Lord, make me an instrument of thy peace. Where there is hatred, let me sow love; where there is injury, pardon; where there is doubt, faith; where there is despair, hope; where there is darkness, light; and where there is sadness, joy.

"O, Divine Master, grant that I may not so much seek to be consoled as to console; to be understood as to understand; to be loved as to love; for it is in giving that we receive; it is in pardoning that we are pardoned; and it is in dying that we are born to eternal life."

3 The Sexual Revolution

In 1956 a Harvard sociologist, Pitirim Sorokin, wrote a book called *The American Sex Revolution*. He pointed to the "odd revolution" that has taken place in America—odd in that it has not involved a class struggle, a civil war, or any of the outward features of most revolutions. Writing as a sociologist, Sorokin called attention to the drastic change that has taken place in the attitudes and actions of Americans concerning sex. He made this observation about the importance of this revolution: "In spite of its odd characteristics, this sex revolution is as important as the most dramatic political or economic upheaval. It is changing the lives of men and women more radically than any other revolution of our time."[1]

In the years since 1956 the sex revolution has grown, not diminished. In fact, the expressions of this revolution that seemed so shocking in the middle Fifties now seem tame by comparison with what has taken place since then.

Many Christians are uncertain about how to respond to this sweeping revolution. Some Christians have been swept along by the revolution to the point of adopting the outlook and sometimes even the actions of sexual revolutionaries. At the other extreme, some Christians have reacted negatively to everything about the sexual revolution. Others seem determined not even to admit that a revolution is taking place. Still others believe that the revolution offers Christians both a challenge and an opportunity—an opportunity to affirm some basic truths about sex and a challenge to oppose pagan immorality.

A Christian response to the sexual revolution should be based on the teachings of the Bible. People who are unfamiliar with the Bible might be surprised to discover that the Bible has much to say about sex. And they would probably be even more surprised to learn that what the Bible says is not a wholesale condemnation of sex. In fact, the Bible begins by describing sex as a part of God's good creation, a part of his purpose for man and woman within the "one flesh" union of marriage (see Gen. 2:18–24). The Bible condemns sexual immorality because it is a perversion of this good purpose of the Creator.

The most extended biblical treatment of the subject is found in 1 Corinthians 5–7. These chapters provide an ideal biblical base for correct Christian attitudes and actions. No Christian is fully prepared to cope with the current sexual revolution until he has an understanding of and commitment to the principles set forth in these chapters.

The ancient sexual revolution. In order to appreciate 1 Corinthians 5–7, we need to recognize the role these chapters played in a "sexual revolution" during the early Christian centuries. We have been referring to the sexual revolution of our own time, but an equally significant revolution in sexual attitudes and actions took place when Christianity confronted the pagan immorality of the Greco-Roman world.

There were many striking contrasts between the teachings of Christ and the ways of the pagan world, but at no point was the contrast any sharper than in the area of sex. The ancient world was steeped in immorality. The moral situation in the area of sex and marriage was dark and chaotic. Yet into this darkness came the preachers of Christ and his way. The deplorable moral conditions were challenged by the Christian emphasis on chastity before marriage and faithful love within marriage. Paul's letter to Corinth reflects the tensions resulting from this confrontation.

The final outcome of this struggle was a revolution in sexual morality. The lax sexual standards of pagan society eventually gave way to the more disciplined attitude of Christianity. This revolution did not take place overnight. It continued through the early Christian centuries, and it gained momentum when the Roman Empire adopted Christianity as its official religion. Under the influence of the Roman Catholic Church of the Middle Ages, the sexual revolution was complete. Acts of immorality still took place in Christendom, but these acts were looked on as sinful by the church and by society.

Unfortunately, however, the Roman Catholic Church overreacted against the immoral excesses of pagan society. Church leaders allowed the pendulum to swing from one false extreme to the other. Many leaders in the centuries after the apostolic age condemned not only sexual immorality but sex itself. In doing this, they departed from the basic biblical teaching that sex is a part of God's good creation.

The official church position in the Middle Ages was that sex is *a necessary evil*—necessary in order to carry on the human race but intrinsically evil in itself. Marriage was looked on as a less holy state than remaining unmarried. The clergy were bound by vows of celibacy. Others were allowed to marry, but all sexual relations except deliberately for the purpose of procreation were considered sinful.

The Protestant Reformation challenged the Roman Catholic view at some points. For example, pastors of Protestant churches were allowed to marry. However, the Protestant Reformation did not bring about a full return to the basic biblical affirmation about sex. The typical Protestant response was to continue to regard sex as a necessary evil. As a result, many Protestant churches adopted an attitude of silence about the sensitive subject. This was particularly true during the Victorian era when sex was not mentioned in polite society.

The modern sexual revolution. About a century ago scientists began to study the subject of sexual attitudes and behavior. Just as in other areas, science challenged the accepted traditional view in the area of sex. And just as in other areas, the foundations of the traditional view began to crumble. Scientists, for example, began to attack the negative attitude toward sex held by many people. They published findings that showed the harmful effects of the belief that sex is only a necessary evil. This attitude was blamed for many emotional problems and for much marital unhappiness. Scientists recommended that sex be accepted as a normal and natural part of life. The public began to pay attention. Unscrupulous men were quick to exploit these new discoveries. And the current sexual revolution began.

The sexual revolution has been aided by many forces at work in the twentieth century. The social upheavals—particularly the many wars have speeded up the process. The mobility of modern society has uprooted people from familiar surroundings and exposed them to many temptations. The advances of science in controlling human conception and in combating veneral disease have removed other deterrents to greater sexual freedom. All these factors have brought about the currently popular attitudes toward sex. The church's views on sex no longer control society. Many people are in open revolt against what they consider Christian teachings about sex and marriage.

The Christian response. David Mace is well known for his wide experience in marriage and family counseling. As a

Christian, he is anxious for modern believers to cope with the sexual revolution from a biblical point of view. Dr. Mace believes that a revolution in basic attitudes has already taken place: Modern society has approved a new freedom to discuss sex, to study it, and to experiment with it. The question is, "How should Christians respond to this revolution?"[2]

Many Christians would approve a twofold response: On one hand, we can seize this opportunity to reaffirm the biblical view of sex as part of God's good creation. On the other hand, we must condemn—and clearly explain why we condemn—sexual immorality.

The sexual revolution is not all bad. To the contrary, its affirmation that sex is good is much closer to the biblical view than the traditional view that sex is a necessary evil. Christians will be wise if they capitalize on this to reaffirm the biblical meaning of sex—God's plan for a man and a woman to make a total commitment to one another in responsible love.

Unfortunately, the current revolution is swinging the pendulum back toward the same dark and chaotic moral situation that existed before Christ came. A popular modern view is that sex, far from being a necessary evil, is an ultimate good; therefore, it should be expressed freely in whatever ways one chooses. A public affairs pamphlet *Sex and Our Society* correctly observes: "We are said to be moving from sex-denial to sex-affirmation, but it is a devious move. We do not affirm sex as a healthy human drive to be harmonized with other healthy human drives. Our culture insidiously presents it as a stolen sweet, a commercial asset, fun, a weapon, a status symbol, a cure for loneliness and above all, the crowning expression of romantic love."[3]

Herein lies the value of studying 1 Corinthians 5—7. Paul clearly condemned the dark excesses of pagan immorality, but he did so in the context of a positive view of human sexuality. Let us, therefore, turn to a more careful examination of what Paul wrote and of what God can say to us through this portion of his Word.

A Conspiracy of Silence (5:1 to 6:11)

When a person goes to a counselor for help, he often does not talk directly about his real problems. This was true of the Corinthians in their letter to Paul. They wrote Paul and asked for help in certain areas. Among their questions were some questions about marriage. Paul dealt with these questions in chapter 7. However, before dealing with their questions, Paul focused attention on some matters that had not been mentioned in their letter. The apostle's words indicate that these were among the real problems in Corinth. Yet the Corinthians had been silent about these problems, either because they hoped to keep Paul from finding out or because they did not consider these as real problems.

The situation described at the beginning of chapter 5 seems to fall in the latter category. There was a case of gross immorality in the church, but the church had adopted a policy of permissiveness about this. Paul was disturbed by the immorality, but he was even more disturbed by the attitude of the church. The biblical passage in which Paul dealt with this problem provides several striking parallels to the current situation in society and in churches.

A shocking case of immorality. The exact nature of the sin described in 1 Corinthians 5:1 is uncertain. Since the Corinthians were aware of the details, Paul felt no need to be more specific than to write, "A man is living with his father's wife." Since Paul did not refer to this as incest, the woman was probably the man's stepmother, not his mother. Since Paul did not refer to this as adultery, the man's father probably was either dead or divorced. Thus the situation seems to have been this: a man was living with his step-mother. The tense of the verb *living* shows that this was not a single incident, but a continuing affair.

Paul referred to this immorality as "a kind that is not found even among pagans" (5:1). Roman law forbade a son to marry his father's wife, even if the father had died. Paul's words do not mean that this sin was never committed among pagans; he meant that even pagan public opinion would not condone such a sin. This was a stinging rebuke to the Corinthian church because pagan public opinion in the area of sex was notoriously lax. All kinds of sexual sins were freely practiced, and nearly all kinds were condoned by society.

In 1 Corinthians 6:9–10, Paul listed some of the kinds of sinners of his day. Among these he mentioned "the immoral," "adulterers," and "homosexuals." The first word referred originally to prostitutes, but it had come to have a wider application to many forms of immorality. All kinds of sexual sins—including the more specific sins of adultery and homosexuality—were practiced in the ancient world. Sexual vice was laughed at on the stage, and it was condoned by public opinion. Few voices were raised against it. Many ethical teachers even found ways of justifying it. Plutarch, for example, wrote that a wife ought not to be angry with her husband when he visited a prostitute because he was doing this out of respect for her.

Religion was no deterrent to immorality. To the contrary, religion often encouraged it. Many of the gods and goddesses of Greek and Roman religion were notoriously immoral themselves. Their worshipers could hardly be expected to do any better. In some cases, as in the worship of Aphrodite in ancient Corinth, sexual immorality was an actual part of the religion. The temple prostitutes in Corinth served as an official part of the worship of Aphrodite.

When archaeologists uncovered the ancient city of Pompeii, many people were shocked by what they found. This Italian city had been buried by an eruption of Mount Vesuvius in the first century. As a result, the diggers found much of the city just as it was when it was buried. What shocked some people were the clear evidences of an immoral society. In all likelihood, Pompeii was a typical first-century town, no worse than others, certainly no worse than Corinth.

The ruins of Pompeii were first uncovered several generations ago before the current sexual revolution. Many people today would not be shocked by what was found in Pompeii. In fact, some would feel right at home in ancient Pompeii or in ancient Corinth. Many students of history are convinced that the current situation is fast approaching the dark, chaotic moral plight of the first-century world.

The Sexual Wilderness. This is the title of a book on the chaotic condition that exists today in the area of sexual morality. Vance Packard, the author of the book, believes that "sexual wilderness" is more appropriate to describe the situation than "sexual revolution."[4] There are many parallels between the sexual wilderness of today and the sexual wilderness of ancient Corinth.

In 1953 Alfred C. Kinsey published his famous "Kinsey report." John W. Drakeford observes: "The Kinsey reports have probably stirred more controversy and become a more authoritative basis for discussion than any other single piece of research on sex in any period of history."[5] Many people were shocked at the extent of premarital and extramarital sexual relations revealed by the report. At first, some people refused to believe Kinsey. However, later studies have generally tended to confirm Kinsey's findings. In fact, more recent studies indicate a continuing gradual increase in the percentage of people involved in sexual intercourse prior to and outside of marriage.

Few people today would discount such scientific studies. Indeed, the percentages seem lower than we might expect in the light of all the emphasis on sex in our society. If we made our judgments on the basis of the movies and books of today, sexual escapades would seem to be universally practiced. The same thing would be true if we were to make our judgment on the basis of what people say. From a forbidden subject, sex has become a favorite topic of conversation. In some circles, boasting of sexual exploits is a way of gaining acceptance with one's peers. David Mace quotes a college chaplain who summed it up well by saying: " 'When all's said and done, there's more said than done.' "[6]

However, this in itself is frightening. Does a healthy society or a mature person take pride in sexual immorality, even to the point of boasting of make-believe sexual exploits? This is where the real revolution has taken place—in attitudes. Some people in every generation have committed acts of sexual immorality; some have even been notoriously immoral; but now such acts are condoned not only by the offender but also by society itself. More and more people not only condone the acts; they actually applaud the acts. As far as they are concerned, chastity and marital faithfulness are the sins and sexual indulgence is the virtue.

As such ideas gain more general acceptance, the changes in sexual practices may change even more rapidly. The changes up till now have been slow and gradual. However, as David Mace observes: "When the number of people practicing the new pattern becomes a clear majority, the process of change should shift to a higher gear and be accelerated. We are probably approaching this point now in the area of premarital sexual intercourse, and possibly also in that of extramarital intercourse."[7] Many Americans interpret statistics as moral guidelines. Thus, when they believe that most people are practicing sexual immorality, they will conclude that this is the normal and right thing to do. If this happens, the result will be an even more entangled sexual wilderness.

The attitude of the church. Where is the church in this sexual wilderness? Obviously it is caught right in the middle of the wilderness. Church members are Christians, but they are also people who are involved in every level of daily life. Far from being immune to the sexual revolution, Christians are strongly influenced by everything that is going on today.

This was surely true of the Corinthian church in its day. The Corinthians were Christians, but they also were Corinthians. The immoral climate of Corinth was an inescapable influence on their attitudes and actions. Instead of shaping their environment, they were being shaped by it. The world had invaded the church: the actions of some of the Corinthians in the area of sex were no different from those of pagan society. As already noted, the man living with his stepmother was acting even worse than most pagans. This was bad enough, but the attitude of the Corinthians was even worse. Isolated cases of sexual immorality seem almost inevitable, but a wholesale toleration of such acts is a different matter.

Paul was amazed: instead of being concerned, the Corinthians were complacent, even proud (vv. 2,6). Did Paul mean that they were proud *in spite of* this sin? Or were they proud *because of* this sin? If the former was true, Paul meant that even a case of gross immorality had been unable to burst their bubble of arrogant pride. If the latter was true, Paul meant that they actually were proud of what the offending member was doing. This latter interpretation is not completely impossible: according to gnosticism, the flesh is evil and transient; only the soul is good. Some of the Gnostics concluded from this that a person whose soul was saved was free to do as he pleased in the area of the flesh.

Whatever the reason for the attitude of the church, Paul condemned their complacency and their pride.

Paul counseled action; he instructed the church to discipline the offending member. First Corinthians 5:5 is especially difficult to interpret: "You are to deliver this man to Satan for the destruction of the flesh, that his spirit may be saved in the day of the Lord Jesus." Some interpreters assume that "the destruction of the flesh" referred to suffering and/or death. But these words may refer to the destruction of sin's power in the man's life. Paul often used the word *flesh* to refer to a sinful life, not to the literal flesh that is subject to suffering and death. Raymond Brown comments: "Probably Paul means that once outside the church the sinner will reflect on his wrong-doing and curb the sin-centered way of life which is characteristic of *flesh*, life without God. Penitent, he will then seek forgiveness and anticipate final redemption."[8]

Discipline is seldom practiced today. In excusing ourselves, we generally say that since all of us are sinners, none of us should judge anyone else. Yet Paul wrote to some very imperfect Christians (see 3:1–4) and told them to discipline a man guilty of gross immorality. This was not only for the sake of the church but also for the sake of the man himself.

Neither Pharisaism nor permissiveness. This passage, of course, needs to be studied in the light of other New Testament passages about church discipline. All of these passages emphasize a spirit of Christian compassion that avoids the equally false extremes of Pharisaism and permissiveness. This can provide a basic guideline to the proper Christian attitude toward the sexual revolution.

Both Jesus and Paul considered excommunication an extreme measure to be taken only after all else had failed. Galatians 6:1 expresses one of the earlier stages of church discipline: "Brethren, if a man is overtaken in any trespass, you who are spiritual should restore him in a spirit of gentleness. Look to yourself, lest you too be tempted." And even when all else fails and extreme measures are necessary, the purpose always should be redemptive.

In 1 Corinthians 6:11, after Paul reminded the Corinthians of some of the terrible sins practiced by men outside the kingdom, he wrote: "And *such were some of you.* But you were washed, you were sanctified, you were justified in the name of the Lord Jesus Christ and in the Spirit of our God." The ethical demands of Christianity are based on our experience of God's grace. While condemning the evil effects of sexual immorality, Christians can never afford to do so in an arrogant, self-righteous spirit. At best, we are only saved sinners.

Follow the example of Jesus as seen in his dealing with the adulterous woman (see John 8:1–11). Jesus neither *condemned* the woman nor *condoned* her sin. Instead he offered forgiveness and acceptance that placed upon her the greatest of all demands—"Go, and sin no more" (John 8:11, KJV).

If we follow Christ's example, we will avoid the negative, condemnatory spirit of the Pharisees. On the other hand, we will also avoid the permissive attitude of the Corinthian church. Allowing a person to go on in his sins is neither the loving nor the Christian thing to do. The same thing could be said of society: allowing society to go down a path toward ruin is neither loving nor Christian.

Too many Christians and churches are guilty of a conspiracy of silence in the area of sex. We have allowed all the other voices in society to present their views; yet by our silence we have deprived many people—even many in the churches—of basic Christian and biblical guidelines in this crucial area of life. Advocates of silence point out that sex is a very private and personal matter; therefore sex should not be mentioned outside the home. Others point out that sex is a controversial topic that should be left alone by churches. Sex is controversial; but like other controversial issues, it is a vital issue that we cannot afford to avoid.

Can we afford to leave the field to the advocates of the new paganism? Do we not owe our society a clear Christian witness to the biblical view of sex and marriage? Do not Christian parents need guidance so that they in turn can help their children? Do not Christian youth need a forum where they can seek and find Christian help in this vital area of life?

Personally, I agree with David Mace when he says, "The 'conspiracy of silence' must end. Everywhere else the open forum on sex prevails. So it must be in the Church also."[9] I also agree with Mace's view that the Christian response to the sexual revolution must be based on biblical teachings. That is one purpose of this book, and specifically of this chapter. Therefore, let us consider Paul's explanation as to why sexual immorality is wrong and why sex in marriage is right and good.

Why Sexual Immorality Is Wrong (6:12-20)

"But why is it wrong?" This question is being asked today, especially by the young. The day is past when the churches can be content to make thundering prohibitions against the evils of sexual immorality. People today want to know what lies back of the prohibitions. Youth and adults—outside and inside the churches—are asking for an answer to the question, "Why is it wrong?"

Sometimes the question is asked in church youth groups. Some leaders try to evade the question, and some even try to make the youth ashamed for asking the question. Wise leaders, however, see in this question an opportunity to present the Christian view of sex.

There will always be the need for clear pronouncements against immorality, but there is also the need to explain what lies back of these pronouncements. Tragically, many Christians—youth and adults—do not know why sexual immorality is wrong. They have heard warnings against it, but they do not know the basis for the warnings. This often makes them easy prey for the subtle propaganda of the world.

First Corinthians 6:12–20 answers the question, "Why is sexual immorality wrong?" Some of the people in Corinth were defending immorality. Paul answered them by setting forth a biblical view of sex that relates sexuality to the total human personality. This makes these verses among the most up-to-date and important verses in the Bible.

Is sex a moral issue? In some translations, parts of verses 12–13 are enclosed in quotation marks: "All things are lawful for me." "Food is meant for the stomach and the stomach for food." Paul quoted what some of the Corinthians were saying to defend their sexual practices.

One line of defense was to say, "All things are lawful for me." In other words, "I am free from any law that prohibits sexual immorality." Possibly, some of the Corinthians were basing this claim on a perversion of Paul's own teaching. Paul preached and taught that a man is saved by grace through faith, not by keeping the Old Testament law. He thus spoke of believers as being "not under law but under grace" (Rom. 6:14). Some of the Corinthians were interpreting Paul to mean that a Christian can disregard the moral law of God.

This is surely not what Paul meant. The apostle was caught between two false extremes—legalism and libertinism. The legalists taught that a man can be justified by keeping the law of God. The libertines taught that a saved man can do as he pleases. Paul preached grace to the legalists and responsibility to the libertines. And each group twisted what Paul said in order to suit their own purposes.

In 1 Corinthians 6:12 Paul responded briefly but effectively to the libertines: " 'All things are lawful for me,' but I will not be enslaved by anything." Freedom without responsibility leads not to freedom, but to a new form of bondage. (Paul elaborated on this idea of responsible freedom in 1 Corinthians 8–10.)

Some of the Corinthians were defending their sexual laxness by saying, 'Food is meant for the stomach and the stomach for food' (v. 13). This may reflect a gnostic-like attitude toward the flesh. The Gnostics taught since sex is a part of the evil flesh, a person whose soul is saved can do as he pleases in this area. Or the background of the statement in verse 13 may have been the difference between Jewish and Christian food laws. The Jews had certain clean and unclean foods; eating an unclean kind of food was a moral issue. Jesus led his followers to see that all foods are clean (see Mark 7:19; Acts 10:15); therefore eating is not a moral issue. Some of the Corinthians were arguing that sex and hunger are in the same category: both are functions of the flesh; neither is a moral issue.

Whatever the background of verse 13, Paul's response shows that the Corinthians were comparing sexual relations to eating. To paraphrase what they were saying: "Food is meant for the stomach and the stomach for food; in the same way sex is meant for the body and the body for sex."

The "Playboy" philosophy. Is it not striking how similar this rationale is to the philosophy proposed by the modern advocates of sexual freedom? Some of the presuppositions are different, but two similar points are made by those who have rejected the Christian view:

1. We are free from any absolute moral law that dictates sexual behavior.
2. Sex is a physical drive that should be satisfied just like any other physical need.

As has already been noted, the former of these ideas is the basis for the current sexual revolution. One authority gives this explanation: *"There is a profound difference between someone who breaks the rules and someone who does not accept the rules.* One is a transgressor; the other is a revolutionary."* He goes on to explain how this applies to the sexual revolution: "The last generation—a sizable minority of it—broke the rules of sexual morality and in particular the rule of premarital chastity, but clandestinely and with great guilt. The members of this generation—a good many of them—simply do not accept the rules any longer. Whether they themselves wish to engage in the forbidden acts is immaterial. Many of them don't wish to. But they challenge the validity of the law—and that is revolution."[10]

Today's sexual revolutionaries not only refuse to feel guilty about immoral acts; they actually defend them as right and good. They even go so far as to attack the church as the real villain in the area of sex. According to them, complete sexual freedom leads to joy and fulfilment, but any kind of sexual discipline, such as confining sex to marriage, leads to repression and unhappiness. Sexual immorality thus is given a new respectability, and Christianity is thrown on the defensive.

This philosophy of free sexual expression is supposed to be based on established scientific facts. This is only partially true: it is based on only one aspect of scientific studies—the physical aspect. In spite of equally important scientific evidence that sex is much more than a biological function, many people still think of sex only as a physical drive. As John Drakeford observes: "Little Annie Oakley can blithely sing about 'doing what comes naturally,' and there will be hearty response from a large group who feel their sex drive is artifically frustrated. They argue that sex is a basic, instinctive, biological hunger of much the same quality as hunger for food or drink; so why artificially restrict it?"[11]

Probably the most popular view of sex in America today is the "Playboy" philosophy. This view has been popularized by Hugh Hefner in his *Playboy* magazine. *Playboy* has twenty million readers, mostly men under thirty. Hefner has built a financial empire by promoting his philosophy through *Playboy* magaine. The "Playboy" philosophy has given new status and social respectability to acts that were considered immoral by earlier generations.

Hefner is not apologetic about being a millionaire, but he likes to picture himself as a reformer. He crusades against the Protestant ethic of sex in marriage. He boldly condemns the church's position as "immoral" because it fosters sexual repression. He presents himself as the prophet of sexual freedom and fulfilment.

Hefner's philosophy is based on an interpretation of sex as a biological function, a physical drive man shares with the animals. He puts sex in the same category with other purely biological drives such as eating and sleeping. As such, sexual needs must be satisfied, or all sorts of harmful neuroses and psychoses may result. Therefore, any attempt to restrict sexual expressions is dangerous; sex should be expressed under whatever condition one chooses.

Hefner does not consider sex a moral issue, at least not in traditional terms of morality. At times, Hefner speaks about the morality of sex being determined by the quality and nature of the relationship, but he tends to define "the quality and nature of the relationship" in a typically *Playboy* way:

"It's quite possible . . .for a sexual relationship to be rather casual and for it still to be . . . really quite moral, because, quite simply, I would define morality as that which serves the best interest of man."[12]

Sex and human personality. Notice Paul's response to this kind of perverted view of sex. He denied that sex and hunger are in the same category. The key to Paul's meaning in his use of the word *body*. When Paul spoke of the *body*, he spoke as a Hebrew, for the Hebrews stressed the body as the total being of a man. When Paul spoke of the *body*, therefore, he was thinking of more than the flesh-and-blood mortal body. He was thinking of the body that will share in the resurrected life of Christ (see v. 14). Flesh and blood will not share in the resurrection, but the body will (see 1 Cor. 15:35–50). Food, eating, and the stomach are all connected with the perishable flesh, but sex is a function of the body that will share in eternity.

In other words, Paul used the word *body* to refer to what men today call *personality*. A man's personality is his essential self. His personality is the totality of his relationship to God and others, and what he is within himself. Human sexuality is obviously a biological function, but it is much more than this—it is an integral part of human personality. Raymond Brown thus suggests that a modern reader of 1 Corinthians 6:12–20 will understand Paul's meaning more clearly if he substitutes the word *personality* in most cases where Paul used the word *body*.[13]

Another key to Paul's meaning is his citing of the one-flesh concept of marriage. Corinth was noted for its immorality, including prostitution. Paul wrote: "Do you not know that your bodies are members of Christ? Shall I therefore take the members of Christ and make them members of a prostitute? Never! Do you not know that he who joins himself to a prostitute becomes one body with her? For, as it is written, 'The two shall become one [flesh]' " (6:15–16).

Paul quoted from the account of God's creation of man and woman. God created them and brought them together. Genesis 2:24 records this significant principle about man and woman: "Therefore a man leaves his father and his mother and cleaves to his wife, and they become *one flesh.*" In his teaching about marriage, Jesus also quoted Genesis 2:24 (see Matt. 19:6). So Paul was stating a key biblical truth when he referred the Corinthians to this principle. This one-flesh concept is the most significant biblical principle regarding human sexuality. It is based on the nature of man and woman and on the divine purpose for human life.

Derrick Sherwin Bailey magnifies this concept in his book *The Mystery of Love and Marriage.* He sees this as a key factor in defining sexuality in terms of personality. Commenting on the meaning of Genesis 2:24, Bailey writes: "Although the union of 'one flesh' is a physical union established by sexual intercourse, . . . it involves at the same time the whole being and affects personality at the deepest level. It is a union of the entire man and the entire woman."[14]

In other words, God made sex as the way whereby one person makes a total commitment of himself to another person in an atmosphere of responsible love. Sexual immorality is wrong because it perverts this purpose of sex. Sex, therefore, is an inescapable moral issue because it involves the whole personality—how a person commits himself, how he relates to others, and ultimately how he relates to God.

This is what Paul meant by quoting Genesis 2:24 in connection with his condemnation of a man's sexual relations with a prostitute. This and other kinds of casual relations are a complete perversion of God's good purpose. Commenting on Paul's words, Bailey writes: "Sexual intercourse, although an act in which the whole man and the whole woman engage, is nevertheless without meaning unless it consummates a true love. . . . In their coming together they either affirm or deny all that sexual intercourse means. In one case they become knit together is a mysterious and significant *henosis* [union] and fulfil their love as husband and wife; in the other they merely enact a hollow, ephemeral, diabolical parody of marriage which works disintegration in the personality and leaves behind a deeply-seated sense of frustration and dissatisfaction."[15]

So long as no one is hurt. Most advocates of sexual freedom have only one rule in their moral code for sex: "Any sexual relationship is permissible *so long as no one is hurt.*" They are especially proud of the qualifying words at the end.

This makes their moral code sound noble—even compassionate, but it is untrue and unrealistic. If sex were only a physical function, this might be an adequate moral code. But since sex involves the total commitment of human personality in responsible love, this moral code is self-contradictory. The problem is that *casual sexual affairs do hurt people.* The fun morality of the "Playboy" philosophy is not always so much fun. Promiscuous sex leaves deep scars on human personality.

Casual sexual relations are immoral because persons are treated as objects to be used, not persons to be loved. In many such relations, one of the persons involved does not consider the relation so casually as the other does. In such a case, this person is exploited, leaving scars of guilt and frustration.

For example, some of Hefner's cast-off bunnies have admitted that they have experienced such feelings as loss of identity and personhood. In a sermon on "Christ and the 'Playboy' Philosophy," Donald B. Strobe said: "It is significant that 'Playboy's' first 'Playmate' was Marilyn Monroe, whose nude picture Hefner purchased for $300 to start his magazine in 1953. We all remember her tragic end when she took her own life because, as she said so many times: 'I never felt like a person—only an object.' "[16]

But what about the modern "liberated" couple who want only a casual relationship? Each agrees not to seek a lasting relationship nor to make any claims on one another. Advocates of sexual freedom want to know, "What's wrong with this?"

This is prostituting to a lesser purpose the means for expressing deep love. Are such people capable of anything other than a superficial relationship? Do not such casual affairs cripple people for sharing and expressing real love— deep, mature, responsible love? Norman Vincent Peale quotes a surgeon's comment about such distortions of sex's true purpose: "It's like using a scalpel for some trivial purpose like cutting out paper dolls. You can cut out the paper dolls, all right, but you can't later do surgery with it.' "[17]

Harvey Cox makes this telling charge against the "Playboy" philosophy: "Playboy and its less successful imitators are not 'sex magazines' at all. They are basically antisexual. They dilute and dissipate authentic sexuality by reducing it to an accessory, by keeping it at a safe distance."[18]

This is what John W. Drakeford meant when he titled his book *The Great Sex Swindle*.The advocates of sexual freedom promise happiness and fulfilment, but this is a lie. Sexual immorality does not deliver what it promises, and it actually keeps a person from finding the freedom, joy, and fulfilment of sex as God intended.

Sex and Marriage (7:1-40)

From C. S. Lewis' imaginative brain came *The Screwtape Letters,* a series of letters from an experienced tempter

Screwtape to an apprentice tempter Wormwood. In one of the letters, Screwtape discussed the subject of human sexuality as a potential area of temptation. He advised Wormwood: "Never forget that when we are dealing with any pleasure in its healthy and normal and satisfying form, we are, in a sense, on the Enemy's [God's] ground. I know we have won many a soul through pleasure. All the same, it is His invention, not ours. He made the pleasures: all our research so far has not enabled us to produce one. All we can do is to encourage the humans to take the pleasures which our Enemy has produced, at times, or in ways, or in degrees, which He has forbidden."[19]

Lewis thus underscored the clear biblical teaching that human sexuality is part of God's good creation. Paul reaffirmed this truth in 1 Corinthians 7. However, the manner in which Paul expressed this affirmation has often been misunderstood. In fact, Paul's teachings in 1 Corinthians have been used by some to undermine the very truth he was affirming. Therefore, we should be all the more careful as we study this important chapter.

In 1 Corinthians 7 Paul was responding to certain questions raised by the Corinthians themselves. Judging from what Paul wrote, these seem to have been some of the questions they asked: Should a Christian get married? Should a widowed Christian remarry? Should a Christian remain married, especially to a non-Christian? Should married Christians have sexual relations?

The nature of these questions shows that there were two basic kinds of misunderstandings of Christian teachings about sex. On one hand, there were the advocates of free sexual expression; Paul dealt with their misunderstanding in chapters 5–6. The opposite view—that sex itself is evil—was dealt with in chapter 7.

The gnostic teaching that flesh is evil could have led to

both kinds of misunderstandings. The sensualist reasoned like this: since flesh is evil and sex is a part of the flesh, it does not matter how one expresses himself sexually. The ascetic began with the same presupposition, but he reached a different conclusion: since flesh is evil and sex is a part of the flesh, we must have nothing to do with sex.

Marriage and celibacy. Some of the Corinthians were saying, "It is well for a man not to touch a woman." That is, they were advocating celibacy. Paul had mixed emotions about this statement. On one hand, he personally preferred to remain unmarried. On the other hand, he did not agree with the reason the ascetics had for remaining unmarried. Therefore, Paul expressed a strong personal preference for celibacy, but he acknowledged that marriage is normal and right for most people.

Students of Paul debate whether or not the apostle had ever been married. We do not have evidence to settle this debate. He may have been a widower, or he may have been a bachelor. What is clear is that Paul was unmarried when he wrote to the Corinthians, and he expressed a strong preference for remaining so. He even advised unmarried and widowed Christians to remain unmarried (see vv. 8–9, 39–40) ; but he based this advice on his view of Christian service, not on his view of human sexuality (see vv. 32–35) .

In Jesus' teachings on marriage, the Lord acknowledged that some of his followers would choose—as Paul did—to remain unmarried for the sake of service in God's kingdom (see Matt. 19:10–12) . But Jesus—like Paul—recognized marriage as the normal course for a man and a woman: " 'Have you not read that he who made them from the beginning made them male and female, and said, "For this reason a man shall leave his father and mother and be joined to his wife, and the two shall become one [flesh]" ' " (Matt. 19:4–5) .

In spite of Paul's personal preference for celibacy he

never taught that marriage is wrong. To the contrary, he wrote, "If you marry, you do not sin" (1 Cor. 7:28). And Paul was very clear on this point: when a couple marries, the marriage must be physically consummated: "The husband should give to his wife her conjugal rights, and likewise the wife to her husband. For the wife does not rule over her own body, but the husband does; likewise the husband does not rule over his own body, but the wife does" (1 Cor. 7:3–4). This command is consistent with the biblical principle of the one-flesh union of husband and wife in marriage.

These words were directed especially to those in Corinth who had decided to remain married but to refrain from sexual relations in marriage. From a biblical point of view, such a practice makes a mockery of marriage by denying the one-flesh basis for mutual commitment to one another.

Paul was willing to make only one slight concession to the ascetics, but he made it plain that this was a concession, not a command. Some of the married Corinthians wanted to refrain from sexual relations. So Paul wrote: "Do not refuse one another except perhaps by agreement for a season, that you may devote yourselves to prayer; but then come together again, lest Satan tempt you through lack of self-control. I say this by way of concession, not of command" (1 Cor. 7:5–6). Even in making this concession, Paul added two strong qualifications: (1) it is to be *for only a season;* and (2) it is to be *by mutual consent.* Anything else would be both selfish (in denying the spouse his or her conjugal rights) and dangerous (in laying one or both open to temptation).

Unfortunately, Paul was quoted by later Christian leaders to support their view that sex is at best a necessary evil. This was unfair to Paul, who had no sympathy with this gnostic view of sex. In 1 Timothy 4:3, Paul warned against false teachers "who forbid marriage." As early as the second century, some Christian couples were living together in a kind of platonic marriage in which no sexual relations were involved. This kind of relationship was supposed to demonstrate their self-control and spirituality. Paul's words in 1 Corinthians 7:3–6 should have been enough to show the folly of such parodies of marriage.

Some commentators are convinced that the difficult passage in 1 Corinthians 7:36–38 reflects such spiritual marriages in first-century Corinth. James Moffatt, for example, translates verse 36: "If a man considers that he is not behaving properly to the maid who is his spiritual bride, if his passions are strong and if it must be so, then let him do what he wants—let them be married; it is no sin for him."[20] According to Moffatt, this kind of spiritual marriage was one of the problems in Corinth. This is possible, but the strong objection to this interpretation of verse 36 is what Paul said in verse 38: whatever the situation in verse 36, Paul expressed a personal preference that the couple remain unmarried. How could the same man who wrote verses 3–6 advise a married couple to live together without sexual relations?

The Greek of verse 36 literally says, "If any one thinks he is not behaving properly toward *his virgin* . . . " The Revised Standard Version assumes that the situation was that of an engaged couple; therefore the word *virgin* is interpreted as "betrothed." This interpretation emphasizes that the most natural way to understand verse 36 is to assume that the man mentioned in the first part of the verse is also the man mentioned in the latter part of the verse. The King James Version assumes that the situation is that of a father trying to decide whether or not to give permission for his virgin daughter to marry. This interpretation emphasizes the difference in meaning between the Greek word for "marry" in verse 36 and the word for "give in marriage" in verse 38. Either of these interpretations would fit the context, for Paul here only reaffirmed what he had written earlier: remaining unmarried was personally preferable to him, but getting married is no sin.

Married for how long? In verses 10–16, Paul dealt with the question, Should a Christian remain married, especially to an unbeliever? Verses 10–11 contain clear instructions to a Christian married to another Christian: they should remain together as husband and wife. Paul had the clear teaching of Jesus as his authority for this teaching (see Matt. 19:3–9). Verses 12–16 refer to a mixed marriage, involving a Christian and a non-Christian. In this case Paul could not quote a teaching of Jesus, but he gave his own authoritative opinion as an apostle.

Verses 12–16 present two difficult problems of interpretation. One problem is verse 14. Paul advised Christians to remain married to their unbelieving spouses. Then he spoke of the unbelieving partner being "consecrated" by the union, and he referred to their children being "holy" (v. 14). Some commentators believe that Paul had in mind some kind of automatic spiritual benefit—perhaps even salvation—that comes from being married to a Christian or through being born into a home where one parent is a Christian. This interpretation is unlikely, for it contradicts the whole tenor of Paul's teachings. More likely, verse 14 was Paul's way of declaring that the marriage is a real marriage. Some Christians were wondering, Can this be a real marriage if my spouse is not a Christian? Paul's answer was that the marriage is real and any children born of the union are legitimate (not "unclean" but "holy").

Therefore, Paul advised Christians to remain married. Elsewhere, he implied that unmarried Christians should marry only Christians. (See 2 Cor. 6:14; this is also the probable meaning of 1 Cor. 7:39, "only in the Lord.") But when a married person is converted, he should remain married. Of course, if the non-Christian takes the initiative in separating, a Christian has little choice except to separate (v. 15).

Verse 16 is the second difficult verse in the passage. One interpretation sees this as a defense of marital harmony, which is closely tied to verse 15. According to this view, Paul was saying in substance: "God has called us to marital peace. So if the unbelieving spouse is determined to leave, let him go. For what hope do you really have of winning him to the Lord? It is better to let him go than to live together in a state of constant tension and strife." The other interpretation sees verse 16 as a reason for remaining married, closely tying verse 16 to verses 12–14. According to this view, Paul's meaning was: "There will be inevitable tensions in any mixed marriage. But stay together if at all possible because there is always the possibility that your unbelieving spouse may be saved by your Christian life and witness." (See 1 Pet. 3:1–2.)

The Christian view of sex and marriage. The Christian view of sex and marriage is based on the biblical definition of the purpose of human sexuality—the mutual and total commitment of a man and a woman in responsible love. This explains, for example, why the Bible never looks on sex, as some Christians have, as a necessary evil; instead human sexuality is seen as one of God's good gifts to mankind, providing not only for procreation but also for the joy and fulfilment of married love. Those who have a negative view of sexuality cannot quote Paul for support.

The Christian view of sexuality also explains why the Bible teaches that marriage should be a lifetime union of husband and wife. Whatever the exact meaning of verse 16, Paul's main point in verses 12–16 is clear: marriage is a lifetime union. This biblical affirmation is closely related to the teaching that sex involves a mutual and total commitment of two persons in responsible love. Such a commitment ideally involves a lifetime union of husband and wife. In a day when marriage is considered by many to be little more than a tentative agreement, these biblical affirmations need to be clearly proclaimed and explained.

Christianity has insisted that marriage is the only proper setting for sexual fulfilment. Under the impact of the sexual revolution, many people are demanding to know why Christians insist on confining sex to marriage. The answer goes back again to the biblical view of the purpose of sex: mutual and total commitment of a man and a woman *in responsible love*. This is the reason the Bible condemns premarital and extramarital sexual relations. How can anything but marriage express what is meant by "responsible love"? How else can the man and the woman be completely responsible to and for one another? How else can they each assume full responsibility for any results of their mutual and total commitment?

The biblical definition of "responsible love" is *marriage*. Those who practice sex before and outside of marriage are acting irresponsibly. Adultery and fornication are wrong because of the harm done to people's lives. In addition, sex is robbed of the joy and fulfilment possible only in responsible love.

Consider, for example, the persons who become involved in an adulterous relationship. Is there any way to begin to measure the potential damage to people's lives by this sin? The harm and hurt spread out in all directions, touching many lives. No one can ever say of the sin of adultery, "It's my business what I do; I'm hurting no one but myself."

And what of sex before marriage? The title of Evelyn Duvall's book poses the question asked by many people,

Why Wait Till Marriage? Some people argue that premarital sex is good preparation for later sexual adjustment in marriage. Evelyn Duvall presents the case for waiting till marriage: "Numerous studies over the past thirty years find premarital chastity associated with both engagement success and marital adjustment. . . . In general, premarital chastity is a favorable beginning for a marriage, for one's own marriage adjustment, and for the happiness of one's marriage partner."[21]

Norman Vincent Peale tells of a young college student who wrote home about the casual sexual relations among her classmates. She wrote: " 'They make it all sound so natural and so inevitable that there are times when I wonder what I'm waiting for.' " Her father answered her letter in this way: " 'I think I can tell you in six words what you are waiting for. *You are waiting to be free.* Free from the nagging voice of conscience and the gray shadow of guilt. Free to give all of yourself, not a panicky fraction. Some deep instinct in you knows what a tremendous experience your first complete union with another person can be—and that same instinct keeps telling you not to blur it, waste it, make it small.' "[22]

4 When Is a Man Free?

Several groups of college students were given a list of eighteen values. Each student was asked to rearrange the list in the order of personal importance. The list included the following values: a comfortable life, an exciting life, a sense of accomplishment, a world at peace, a world of beauty, equality, family security, freedom, happiness, inner harmony, mature love, national security, pleasure, salvation, social recognition, self respect, true friendship, and wisdom. When the results were tabulated, *freedom* stood at the top of the list; more students placed greater priority on freedom than on any other value.[1]

Without a doubt, freedom is a popular idea. People of all ages place great value on freedom. But, strangely enough, freedom is not easy to define. It often means all things to all men.

One of the most popular definitions was that given by Franklin Delano Roosevelt in his famous "Four Freedoms" speech to Congress on January 6, 1941. Much of the rest of the world was already at war when the President proposed that the goal of American policy be the establishment throughout the world of freedom of speech, freedom of religion, freedom from want, and freedom from fear.

This was and is a noble goal, but something more basic lies back of the four freedoms. Judge Learned Hand spoke of this more basic freedom in a speech on "The Spirit of Liberty." He recognized that political freedom depends ultimately on a spirit in the lives of citizens. He said:

"Liberty lies in the hearts of men and women; when it dies there, no constitution, no law, no court can save it; no constitution, no law, no court can even do much to help it. When it lies there it needs no constitution, no law, no court to save it."[2]

It is no coincidence that the Bible has exerted a strong influence on the shaping of American political freedom. The Bible is a source book on freedom. Although the Bible provides no model for political freedom, it points toward that freedom of spirit which is the basis for any form of true liberty. Many of the people of Bible times lived under the reigns of political tyrants, but they lived and acted as free men—free under the yoke of allegiance to God. (Imagine what more they could have done if they had lived in an era of political freedom!)

The Bible contains several famous passages that deal with the subject of freedom. Many people remember the famous words of Jesus: "If you continue in my word, you are truly my disciples, and *you will know the truth, and the truth will make you free*" (John 8:31–32). The entire passage—especially verses 31–36—speaks of the inner freedom of spirit made possible through Christ: "So if the Son makes you free, you will be free indeed" (John 8:36).

One cannot speak of the Bible's teachings on freedom without mentioning Paul's letter to the Galatians. Paul defended freedom in Christ: "For freedom Christ has set us free; stand therefore, and do not submit again to a yoke of slavery" (Gal. 5:1). The apostle also stressed the responsibility of freedom: "For you were called to freedom, brethren; only do not use your freedom as an opportunity for the flesh, but through love be servants of one another" (Gal. 5:13).

First Corinthians 8–10 is another Bible passage bearing on the subject of freedom. In these chapters, Paul dealt with a specific problem in the Corinthian church—meat sacrificed to idols. Although this problem has no parallel in our society, the principles of freedom and responsibility explained by Paul are as up-to-date as the modern quest for freedom.

How Free Am I? (8:1–13)

"My freedom to poke out my fist ends where my neighbor's nose begins." This is one way to state an inescapable principle of human freedom: my freedom is limited by the rights and needs of others.

This is true of political freedom. We live in a free society, but it is not a lawless society. Ideally, the laws should guarantee the greatest measure of freedom and self-expression for the greatest number of people. Therefore, in order to accomplish this goal, the laws must set limits on an individual's freedom to do as he pleases. No person is free to disregard the rights of others. This would result in anarchy, not freedom.

This principle of freedom limited by the rights and needs of others is set forth by Paul in 1 Corinthians 8. However, Paul's meaning probes much deeper than the tension between individual liberties and civil rights in a democratic society. Paul's words encompass the whole area of interpersonal relations—in the church, in the home, in society.

Meat sacrificed to idols. First Corinthians 8:1 begins Paul's discussion of another of the questions asked by the Corinthians in their letter to Paul. (See 1 Cor. 7:1.) The problem related to "food offered to idols." This was not the problem of ceremonially clean and unclean foods, which presented a problem to some Jewish Christians (see Acts 10:14). Neither was it the question of whether or not to eat meat of any kind (see Rom. 14:2). The problem at

Corinth was whether or not to eat the meat of an animal that had been sacrificed in a pagan temple.

Pagan worship, like Jewish worship, involved the sacrifice of animals. Only a small portion of the animal was actually sacrificed; the rest was used in various ways. A portion of the meat was eaten by the priests of the temple. The rest of it might be taken home by the worshiper, it might be sold in the marketplace, or it might be eaten in a feast of worship in the temple. The Corinthian Christians, therefore, could come into contact with this meat in various ways.

A non-Christian friend might invite a Christian to a meal in his home. Very likely, the meat served at the meal would be meat from an animal sacrificed to idols. Should a Christian accept such an invitation; and if so, should he eat the meat?

When a Christian went into the marketplace, he found it almost impossible to buy meat that had not been sacrificed to idols. Many of the butcher shops were built adjacent to a temple; in such a case the shopper could be almost certain that the animal had been sacrificed. And he had no assurance that meat purchased elsewhere was not also from a sacrificed animal. Since the best animals were usually sacrificed, the best meat sold by the butchers was usually "food offered to idols."

Many public banquets were held in pagan temples. This included not only official times of idol worship but also many social affairs. Many public banquets began by offering the animal to the patron deity of the temple. Some people who did not believe in idols attended these banquets as purely social functions. Christians had to decide whether or not they should ever take part in such banquets.

The truth that sets men free. Judging from what Paul

wrote, the Corinthians were divided on this issue. Some of them took the position that eating meat of any kind was not a moral issue. Others, however, believed that eating meat sacrificed to idols was a sinful act.

The former group based their position on their knowledge that idolatry is meaningless because there is only one true God. Therefore, they reasoned, there can be no harm in eating meat sacrificed to an idol. Paul was in essential agreement with their contention that " 'an idol has no real existence' " and " 'there is no God but one' " (vv. 4–6). He also was willing to agree that food is not a moral issue. He wrote in verse 8: "Food will not commend us to God. We are no worse off if we do not eat, and no better off if we do."

However, Paul was not in complete sympathy with this group. They were proud of their superior knowledge. They looked down on those with scruples about eating meat sacrificed to idols.

Paul warned them that such proud knowledge is deceptive: "We know that 'all of us possess knowledge.' 'Knowledge' puffs up, but love builds up. If any one imagines that he knows something, he does not yet know as he ought to know" (vv. 1–3). The person who is proud of his knowledge reveals how little he really knows. This is true in all areas of knowledge, and it is even more true of the knowledge possessed by a Christian.

Verse 3 shows how completely the proud Corinthians had misunderstood the nature of true knowledge. The most basic kind of knowledge is knowledge of God. This knowledge does not consist of an accumulated knowledge of various truths about God. To the contrary, it consists of a personal knowledge of God. Such knowledge is not a human attainment of which to be proud, but a gift of grace for which to be grateful. When Paul spoke of our knowledge of God, he always based this on God's prior knowledge of us. The last part of verse 3 is reminiscent of Galatians 4:9: Paul had written that the Galatians had "come to know God," but he quickly corrected himself by adding, "or rather *to be known by God.*"

When Jesus made his famous promise about the truth that sets men free (John 8:32), he was not talking about truth as an intellectual attainment. He was talking about personal knowledge of and commitment to God. This, not intellectual knowledge, is the truth that sets men free.

Don't be a stumbling block. Paul had an even more serious warning for the Corinthians: being puffed up by their knowledge was bad enough, but causing their brothers to stumble was even worse. Some of their Christian brothers did not share their liberal views about eating meat sacrificed to idols. Prior to their conversion, many of these scrupulous brothers had worshiped idols. For years they had eaten meat sacrificed to idols as an act of pagan worship. Now they found it difficult to disassociate the food from the idols. They considered it impossible to eat such meat without being guilty of idol worship.

The other group of Corinthian church members, who boasted of their superior wisdom, were proud of their freedom to eat meat sacrificed to idols. But Paul warned: "Take care lest this liberty of yours somehow become a stumbling block to the weak. For if any one sees you, a man of knowledge, at table in an idol's temple, might he not be encouraged, if his conscience is weak, to eat food offered to idols?" (Vv. 9–10.)

How could the weak brother's conscience be hurt by seeing another Christian eating meat sacrificed to idols? Paul spoke of their consciences being "defiled" (v. 7) and "wounded" (v. 12); he even spoke of the persons themselves being "destroyed" (v. 11). The apostle clearly recognized the danger of a person acting contrary to the dictates of his conscience. A conscience is not a perfect measure of what is right or wrong, but a conscience is one vehicle God can use to direct a man's steps. Therefore, acting contrary to conscience is dangerous. This is true even when the act—like eating meat sacrificed to idols—is not evil in itself. If the weak brother goes against his conscience in a matter such as this, he may be emboldened to do so in other areas. In his mind, eating meat sacrificed to idols is part of pagan idolatry. If he goes so far as to eat the meat, he may go all the way and share in the whole system of idolatry—even the pagan, immoral rites.

Paul considered this a serious matter. This was a sin against one's brother in Christ and, therefore, a sin against Christ himself. Christ had died to redeem the brother, and the Lord was joined in a faith-union with the brother. Sinning against the brother, therefore, is the same as sinning against the Lord himself.

The demands of Christian love. In the light of this, Paul stated his own course of action: "Therefore, if food is a cause of my brother's falling, I will never eat meat, lest I cause my brother to fall" (v. 13). Thus Paul exemplified the Christian love he had mentioned in verse 1.

The direct application of this principle is to questions of right and wrong faced by Christians in every generation. In considering such questions, a Christian must ask himself not only, "What effect will this have on me?" but also, "What effect will this have on others?"

For example, consider the problem of beverage alcohol. Many people, including some Christians, claim that beverage alcohol is no more than a harmless social custom. They insist that since alcohol does them no personal harm, they should be free to drink. The biblical basis for total abstinence is found in the two questions asked in the preceding paragraph.

Alcohol is seldom so harmless as most people assume. The principle set forth in 1 Corinthians 6:19–20 applies not only to sexual immorality but also to any other sin against one's body. Many Christians are convinced that this principle of the stewardship of the body applies to beverage alcohol. But let us suppose for a moment that a Christian was sure (which he is not) that beverage alcohol posed no danger to him personally. Would he then be morally justified in exercising his freedom to drink? Not if he takes seriously the teaching in 1 Corinthians 8. Drinking is not something that can be done without exercising some influence on other people, and a Christian must consider the possible harmful effect of his own indulgence. To quote Paul's words from Romans 14:21, "It is right not to eat meat or drink wine or do anything that makes your brother stumble."

The principle taught in chapter 8, however, should not be limited to this direct application; it should also be applied more broadly. The broad principle is this: A Christian's freedom is channeled by the demands of Christian love. He is not free to act only in his own interest; he must also consider the needs of others. In fact, he is actually bound by the needs of others to act on their behalf.

In *Burma Diary,* Paul Geren recorded one occasion when he and two other men were asked to move patients from one hospital ward to another. One of the three men was an agnostic; Geren and the other man were Christians. The three of them had had several discussions about religion. When they arrived at the doorway of the hospital ward, they faced an unpleasant task: the patients were victims of dysentery, and their disease had made the air foul and the whole scene revolting. As they stood there, the agnostic said, "I am very glad at this very moment I am agnostic." Geren explained this strange remark: "Since he did not believe in the love of Christ, he could leave the handling of these dysentery victims to the sweepers. Since his friend did believe in it he was not free to stand by and watch. Nor was I."[3]

What About My Rights? (9:1–27)

The basic meaning of the word "liberty" in 1 Corinthians 8:9 is right or authority; the Corinthians were asserting their *right* to eat the meat. One of the marks of unregenerate man is the assertion of his own rights and privileges. By contrast, Christianity challenges us to subordinate our own rights to a higher cause—allowing the love of Christ to work through us to meet the needs of others.

Paul had stated this principle earlier in his letter in reference to lawsuits among Christians. (See 6:1–8.) Some of the Corinthian church members were involved in court suits with one another before pagan judges. Each party was insisting on his own rights. Paul rebuked this worldly spirit: "To have lawsuits at all with one another is defeat for you. Why not rather suffer wrong? Why not rather be defrauded?" (1 Cor. 6:7). In other words, the Christian thing to do in such a case would be to give up one's rights rather than bring reproach on the cause of Christ.

In 1 Corinthians 8:13 Paul had stated his own commitment to this principle with regard to meat offered to idols. Chapter 9 further illustrates Paul's practice of this principle. For the moment, Paul turned aside from the problem of meat sacrificed to idols and talked instead about another subject familiar to the Corinthians—pay for preachers.

Paying the preacher. A large part of chapter 9 is devoted to a minister's right to expect financial support from a congregation. In the background were two factors in Paul's relation with the Corinthian church: (1) Paul had not taken any pay for his work in Corinth. (2) Some of the Corinthians assumed that this was an indirect admission by Paul that he was not a real apostle.

Thus Paul began by attacking the insinuation that he was not a true apostle. (See vv. 1–6.) The other apostles had received financial support from the Corinthians. Some of them had even received financial support for their wives, who accompanied their husbands. Paul made it plain that he had as much right to such support as any of the other apostles.

Then Paul made some general observations about a minister's right to expect financial support (see vv. 7–11, 13–14). He used several lines of argument to establish this fact:

1. Human analogies—soldier, vine-dresser, shepherd (v. 7).
2. Old Testament law (vv. 8–10).
3. Analogy to the priest sharing in the sacrifice (v. 13).
4. Teaching of Jesus (v. 14; see Luke 10:7).

Paul had earlier referred to himself as a worker in the field at Corinth (3:5–9). As such, he deserved the same support others had received. In fact, he deserved it even more than they, for Paul had been the first to break the ground and sow the seed of the gospel in Corinth. (See vv. 11–12.)

Giving up your rights. Paul might have seemed to be leading up to a payment of back wages. But after establishing his right to expect support, he made a different point: "Nevertheless, we have not made use of this right, but we endure anything rather than put an obstacle in the way of the gospel of Christ" (v. 12).

Why did Paul not accept pay from the Corinthians? The

only clue here is verse 12. The word "obstacle" means literally "an incision." The idea may be that of warfare, when an enemy army tries to destroy bridges and cut roads. Paul did not want to play the role of an enemy who places obstacles in the way of the gospel; to the contrary, he wanted to keep the road open for the advance of the gospel.

Paul's other letters provide some further clues to the Corinthian situation. Paul had accepted pay from the Philippian church while he was at Thessalonica (Phil. 4: 15–16) and later at Corinth (2 Cor. 11:9). He did not accept pay from the people in Thessalonica and in Corinth because he did not want to burden them (1 Thess. 2:9; 2 Thess. 3:8; 2 Cor. 11:7–11). Second Corinthians 11:12 implies that there also was another reason why Paul refused to ask the Corinthians for financial help. Paul had some critics among the Corinthians. If Paul had accepted pay for his work in Corinth, these critics might have used this to try to discredit Paul and his work. Paul was not concerned about any personal affront to him, but he was concerned that this might damage the effectiveness of the gospel message in Corinth.

Paul did not want the Corinthians to misunderstand his reason for bringing up the subject of his right to financial support. Verse 15 explains that Paul was not implying that they should begin to support him now; to the contrary, Paul had rather die than to lose his right to preach the gospel without pay. Verses 16–18 elaborate on this right: Paul's choice was not between preaching or not preaching; it was between preaching *for pay* or preaching *without pay*. He did not have any option about preaching, for he was under the compulsion of a divine mandate to preach the gospel. Like Jeremiah, Paul had a fire shut up in his bones that would not allow him to quit preaching (see Jer. 20:9). If the matter were wholly a matter of Paul's own choice (to preach or not to preach), he could rightly have expected a reward; but as it was, he was only a servant acting under divine orders.

Paul had to preach, but he did not have to preach without pay. He had the right to expect pay, but he had chosen to give up this right in Corinth. Why did he give it up? He did so for the sake of his commitment to something he considered more important than his own individual needs—the advance of the gospel.

A Christian is free in Christ. He has certain rights and privileges. If he chooses, he can assert his rights and demand all of his privileges. Or he can voluntarily set aside his rights when this contributes to a higher cause. To do the former is to miss the purpose of freedom in Christ. To do the latter is to express the essence of freedom in Christ.

Free for what? Many people think only of the negative aspect of freedom—what we are *free from;* they fail to see the positive aspect of freedom—what we are *free for.* As a Christian, Paul had been set free *from* the power of sin and death; he had been set free *for* the proclamation of the gospel. Verses 1–18 show how he had set aside his right of ministerial support for the sake of the gospel. Verses 19–23 show how he subordinated other areas of his life for the sake of the proclamation of the gospel.

Verse 19 is a key statement of Paul's commitment: "For though I am free from all men, I have made myself a slave to all that I might win the more." This was Paul's evangelistic strategy in a nutshell. He was willing to make whatever personal accommodations were needed to win men to Christ. He wrote, "I have become all things to all men that I might by all means save some" (v. 22).

Because he had experienced the blessings of God's saving grace, Paul felt keenly his obligation to share this gospel with all men. Therefore, he made this his goal—to win men to Christ. In order to attain this goal, he accommodated himself to the situation and needs of others. His own rights and privileges became secondary to his goal of sharing the gospel of salvation.

When Paul preached to the Gentiles, he laid aside his Jewish background and scruples. He did this in order to have the best opportunity of winning Gentiles to faith in Christ. When Paul dealt with Jews, he tried to accommodate himself to Jewish customs and ways, even when he no longer considered them pertinent (see Acts 16:3; 21:20). He did this in order to have the best opportunity of winning Jews to faith in Christ.

James Moffatt points out how Paul's evangelistic strategy of accommodation avoids the pitfalls of two false extremes in evangelization—dogmatism and compromise. At one extreme is dogmatic zeal, which presents Christ in a " 'take or leave it' spirit, without much regard to the particular circumstances of the audience."[4] At the other extreme is compromise, which either denies or ignores convictions in order to make friends and win followers. Critics may have accused Paul of falling into this latter trap, but accommodation is not compromise of principle or conviction. Besides, Paul was always intent on winning men to Christ, not to himself.

Paul's principle of accommodation is very similar to the basic idea in "cultivation witnessing." This approach to witnessing is based on winning a person's friendship in order to win him to Christ. Many people today are suspicious of Christians and churches. Often the only basis for witnessing to such people comes as a result of winning their confidence and friendship.

The obvious danger in this approach is that the Christian may never carry out the witness. The ultimate purpose of winning the person's friendship is to win him to Christ. This does not mean that winning his friendship is only a gimmick. To the contrary, it means that the ultimate goal of genuine Christian concern in any friendship is to win our friends to Christ and to help them reach their full potential in Christ.

This approach to evangelism is always costly to the evangelist. Accommodation costs time, energy, effort, and sometimes much more.

John Duncan was a Scottish Christian of the last century. This skilled linguist and Hebrew scholar was noted also for the depth of his Christian concern. Duncan learned of a man who was dying in an Edinburgh hospital. No one could identify the man nor could they understand the language he spoke. From his appearance, they judged that the man was from one of the Eastern countries. Duncan's linguistic training was in Eastern languages, but even he could not understand the man's dialect. However, John Duncan, speaking in the spirit of Paul, stated his intention: "I will learn his language, that I may tell him about Jesus."[5]

General William Booth, the founder of the Salvation Army, was another man who lived and spoke in the same spirit as Paul. Booth specialized in trying to win those people whom the rest of society largely ignored. He used everything from brass bands to free food in an attempt to win men for Christ. Most of all he used his life, going into the dark places of human sin and misery as a representative of the "Friend of sinners." A few years before his death, Booth was invited to Buckingham Palace. King Edward VII asked the old general to write in his autograph album. Booth wrote the following words:

> Your Majesty,
> Some men's ambition is art,
> Some men's ambition is fame,
> Some men's ambition is gold,
> My ambition is the souls of men.[6]

Freedom involves discipline. Paul anticipated that critics might confuse his principle of accommodation with easy-going compromise. To the contrary, Paul claimed, his approach to winning men involved severe and costly discipline. Paul wanted to be free to serve as a successful fisher of men; this goal demanded the sternest kind of self-discipline. (See vv. 24–27.)

Paul compared himself and other Christians to runners in a race. His point was that Christians must exercise the same kind of self-discipline as successful athletes. The Corinthians were familiar with athletic contests, for the Isthmian Games were held there every two years. Therefore, they understood the rigorous diet and training of Greek athletes. If athletes undergo such discipline for purely earthly goals, how much more should Christians for eternal goals!

Paul also compared himself to a boxer who fights with a purpose. He wrote, "I do not box as one beating the air" (v. 26). This may refer either to shadow boxing or to missing his opponent. In either case, the point is that Paul was in dead earnest. He gave an unusual turn to the analogy by casting himself in the role of his own opponent, "I pommel my body and subdue it" (v. 27). Paul recognized that he was potentially his own worst enemy. His words in Romans 7:13–25 show how egocentricity could paralyze his potential for victorious living and effective service.

Paul did not fear the things most men fear. He did not fear sickness, suffering, persecution, or even death. The only thing he feared was the possibility of failing to fulfil the task God had given to him. Because he knew himself so well, Paul was aware of how easy it would be to fail to do his best for God. Therefore, he practiced rigorous self-discipline.

The attaining of freedom's goals always involves self-discipline. Paul's analogy of the athlete is still appropriate.

No athlete can excel without persistent efforts to stay in shape and in practice. Back of his athletic feats are long hours of exercise and training. A person may have great natural athletic potential, but he will never excel without discipline. On the other hand, many people who are not blessed with great natural potential have been able to excel through careful training and discipline.

Leslie Weatherhead tells of a famous runner who was invited to break training for a wild party. The athlete replied, "I am not free to do what you ask. For if I did what you ask, I should not be free to run."[7]

This principle is built into the fabric of life: the freedom to attain any worthy goal depends on the practice of self-discipline. A physician is free to heal because of his long years of training. A musician is free to produce beautiful music because he spends long hours of disciplined practice. A Christian is free to be an effective witness for Christ because he has disciplined himself to live in such a way as to attain this goal.

When Freedom Becomes Dangerous (10:1–33)

Thus far, in chapters 8—9, Paul has stressed that freedom is a positive concept and that attaining freedom's goals involves discipline. These are valid principles for every area of life. For example, political freedom must be exercised positively and responsibly, or it tends toward one of two deadly dangers—tyranny or anarchy. Both tyranny and anarchy are forms of bondage. Ironically, a free nation is most in danger of losing its freedom when its citizens are concerned about their own rights and privileges, not about others or the nation as a whole.

Part of the problem at Corinth was that many of the Corinthians ignored these important principles. They emphasized the negative, not the positive side of freedom—

what we are free *from,* not what we are free *for.* As a result, they stressed doing as they pleased, not disciplining themselves for a higher purpose. Paul addressed this group in chapter 10.

The danger of false confidence. Judging from what Paul wrote in 1 Corinthians 10:1–22, some of the Corinthians were presuming on their supposed spiritual enlightenment. As a result, they were walking dangerously close to harmful sin. Yet they seemed blissfully unaware of the danger.

In chapter 8, Paul had warned them of the harm they could do to their weaker brothers. In chapter 10, he warned them of the harm they could do to *themselves.* Apparently Paul had in mind their careless attitude toward idolatry. They saw no harm in eating meat sacrificed to idols under any circumstances—even eating in a pagan temple as a part of a formal worship service. They prided themselves in their knowledge that idols are nothing; therefore they considered themselves free to attend these idol feasts for purely social reasons. Irenaeus, a Christian writer of the second century, tells how the Gnostics of his day were always the first to arrive at idol feasts. Something of the same spirit was at work in the Corinthian church in the first century. They insisted on their right to practice their freedom in whatever way they chose.

Paul drew a parallel between the Corinthians and the history of Israel in the wilderness (see vv. 1–12). Like the Israelites, they were presuming on their relation to the Lord; and like the Israelites they were in danger of falling into sin. In verses 6–10, Paul listed five specific sins committed by the Israelites. Each of these applied in some way to the danger of idolatry in Corinth: desiring evil things (v. 6), idolatry (v. 7), immorality (v. 8), putting God to the test (v. 9), and grumbling against God (v. 10).

Verse 12 clearly expresses Paul's warning: "Therefore let any one who thinks he stands take heed lest he fall."

Since the sinking of the *Titantic* on April 14, 1912, this disaster has become a symbol of the danger of false confidence. Blind confidence is seen in the attitude of the *Titantic's* radio operator. A radio operator from a nearby vessel, *The Californian,* tried to warn the *Titanic* of icebergs in the area. The *Titanic* operator responded with these impatient words: "Shut up, shut up! I am busy; I am working Cape Race."[8]

This unconcern was based no doubt on the assumption that the *Titanic* was unsinkable. And besides, the operator was preoccupied with sending and receiving messages about the progress of ships in the Cape Sailing Regatta. Shortly after this, the mighty *Titanic* struck an iceberg, and within a few hours it sank with a loss of fifteen hundred lives.

Flirting with temptation. The words of warning in verse 12 are balanced by words of assurance in verse 13. The latter verse has always been a favorite text for helping Christians cope with temptation. The verse promises that God always provides a way of escape for the Christian being tempted. Unfortunately, men often fail to escape temptation because they are not really looking for a way of escape. As a result, they often flirt with sin and temptation. Instead of earnestly praying, "Lead us not into temptation," they unnecessarily expose themselves to danger.

In verse 14, Paul spelled out what he meant: "Wherefore, my dearly beloved, *flee from idolatry*" (KJV). In 6:18, he had been equally clear in stating the first rule about overcoming temptations to sexual immorality, "Flee fornication" (KJV). This should be the most obvious rule in overcoming any temptation: do not expose yourself to temptation unnecessarily. The Christian's aim should not be to see how close he can come to danger but how far away he can stay.

Verses 14–22 express the real peril Paul had in mind in verses 1–13—the peril of self-indulgence in idol feasts. Some of the Corinthians were claiming that they could take part in idol feasts as a harmless social function. But Paul did not agree. He did not base his objection on the possible harm to a brother of weaker conscience (as he did earlier in chapter 8 and later in 10:23–30); he based his objection in verses 14–22 on the possible harm to the self-confident church member who shared in the idol feast.

In 8:4–6, Paul had stated his belief that an idol is nothing because there is only one true God. However, in 10:14–22, he added another dimension to the problem. idol worship is actually demon worship. When a Christian participates in the Lord's Supper, he is in communion with the Lord. In the same way, Paul claimed, when a person participates in an idol feast, he is in communion with demons. (See Deut. 32:15–18.) Therefore, such worship is completely incompatible with Christian worship: "You cannot drink the cup of the Lord and the cup of demons. You cannot partake of the table of the Lord and the table of demons" (v. 21).

In other words, the danger of idolatry was not just that it diverted worship from the one true God, but that it directed worship toward that which was evil. No doubt, Paul had good reason for his concern. He probably knew of instances when an "enlightened" Christian had attended an idol feast as a purely social occasion, only to become involved again in all the evils associated with pagan idolatry.

Perhaps some of the Corinthians defended their return to the idol feasts as an evangelistic endeavor: like Paul, they were trying to be all things to all men in order to win their old friends. This is the form in which the problem often arises today: a convert who tries to win his former companions may be tempted to return to his old ways. A Christian must be a friend of sinners, but he also must be careful not to become involved in the very sins from which he would deliver others.

Free yet bound. In verses 23–33, Paul summarized and concluded his discussion of the problem of meat sacrificed to idols. Verse 23 reads: " 'All things are lawful,' but not all things are helpful. 'All things are lawful,' but not all things build up." The words *all things are lawful* were probably a quotation from the Corinthians. They used this formula to justify their freedom to eat meat sacrificed to idols, even during an idol feast.

Judging from 1 Corinthians 6:12, some of them also used this formula to condone sexual immorality. Notice the similarity and difference between 10:23 and 6:12, which reads: 'All things are lawful for me,' but not all things are helpful. 'All things are lawful for me,' *but I will not be enslaved by anything.*" The main difference is in the last part of each verse: 10:23 stresses the need to build up fellow Christians; 6:12 warns against the danger of a new kind of bondage for the self-indulgent.

In a sense, 6:12 is an appropriate summary of the danger expressed in 10:1–22, as well as in 6:13–18. When liberty becomes license, the result is a new form of bondage. The person who is concerned only about his own freedom to do as he pleases is in danger of becoming enslaved by his own self-indulgence.

This assertion of personal freedom—apart from the will of God and the needs of others—is what the Bible calls *sin*. This perversion of God-given freedom was the sin of Adam and Eve. The person who insists on interpreting his freedom in this way shows that he knows little about God,

human society, or himself. Sin has an addicting quality. A
Jesus put it, "Every one who commits sin is a slave to sin"
(John 8:34). This is true of all kinds of sin—not only o
such outward sins as sexual immorality and drunkennes
but also of such inward sins as pride and envy. Sin involve
the sinner in a bondage that robs him of the very freedom
and fulfilment he is seeking.

Leslie Weatherhead tells a parable of a mariner who se
sail saying to himself: " 'I am not going to take any notic
of this conventional chart, or this compass, or indeed o
the stars of the heaven. I am free of them all. I am goin
to do what I like. I am going to sail my vessel as I like an
where I like.' " Weatherhead draws the lesson from th
parable: "How grimly the stormy seas would laugh at hin
and how soon he and his ship would find the bottom of th
ocean! It is when he accepts the discipline of the chart, th
advice of the compass, the tyranny—if you like—of th
eternal stars that he finds at last the harbour."[9]

Bound yet free. This parable illustrates both sides o
the paradox of freedom: (1) the person who insists o
doing as he pleases ends up enslaved; (2) the person wh
enslaves himself to a higher cause finds true freedom an
fulfilment. Paul took the latter course: "For though I an
free from all men, I have made myself a slave to al
that I might win the more" (1 Cor. 9:19). This is th
most demanding of all commitments, but it also is the *mo
liberating.*

Weatherhead illustrates this paradoxical nature of Chri
tian freedom by summarizing the message in one of th
poems of Rabindranath Tagore: "The poet picks up
piece of catgut and finds that it is a violin string, but as l
holds it between his finger and thumb, it is all but usele
It is free at both ends, but no music can be made from
in that state. When he fits it to his violin and binds it

both ends and turns the peg until the violin string is taut, then because it is bound, it is free to sing."[10]

"*Free to sing. . . .*" That is the point! It is bound for a purpose and in that purpose is its freedom. Everything depends on worthy goals for freedom.

In his summary statement, Paul mentioned three such goals: the glory of God (v. 31), the strengthening of the church (vv. 23–24, 32), and the conversion of the lost (v. 33). These were the consuming goals of Paul's life.

As a result of this bondage to God and his will, Paul was free to be himself as God intended for him to be. He did not fear men or what men could do to him. Under the most limiting of circumstances, he remained a free man. In the Philippian jail, Paul sang songs of praise to God (Acts 16:25). When he appeared before Agrippa, he pressed the claims of Christ even on the playboy king (Acts 26:29).

It all boils down to a choice between two kinds of bondage—bondage under God's will or bondage under the world's way. We exercise our freedom of choice when we choose one or the other of these forms of bondage.

Jesus' parable of the prodigal son is an excellent illustration of this truth. The prodigal son left home expecting to find freedom as he escaped the limitations of his father's home. But his unlimited self-expression brought him at last to the bondage of the pig pen. He "came to himself" when he realized that he could exchange this undesirable bondage for the bondage of his father's home. Commenting on this parable, Helmut Thielicke writes: "When the son found the father *anew* . . . he realized that he had also found himself in this bond, and therefore had arrived at real freedom. We have only to choose between bondage to the Father, which makes us free, and bondage to the powers of this world, which enslaves us."[11]

5 What About the Church?

Dick Van Dyke has been a favorite entertainer among church-going people—not only because of his obvious talents as an entertainer but also because of his loyalty to his church. When Mr. Van Dyke first became nationally known as an entertainer, churchgoers were pleased to learn that he was a loyal member of the Presbyterian Church, even serving as an elder. As his fame grew, we were glad to see that he remained loyal to his Christian faith and to his church. It was with shock and regret that we learned he had fallen out with the church. " 'No change in my religious point of view,' " Van Dyke told *TV Guide* reporter Dwight Whitney. " 'But the church got a long way from what it was supposed to be doing. It has become arrogant and judgmental of the rest of the human race.' "[1]

A minister was being interviewed on TV. For years he had served as a pastor of several congregations, but he explained that he had given up on the institutional church. He told the interviewer that he had dropped out of the church in order to engage in more relevant social ministries.

A young contestant in a beauty pageant was asked to give an impromptu talk of "What Youth Find Wrong with Institutional Religion." Without hesitation, she launched into her subject and quickly listed several reasons why youth are critical of organized religion.

The church is under attack at all levels of today's society. The criticism comes from inside and outside the church, from the old and the young. Among the most frequent charges are these: irrelevant, inconsistent, out-of-step with the times, untrue to its mission, interested only in self-preservation, unwilling to adapt to new ideas and methods.

Christianity or the church? Part of the criticism reflects a reaction against anything institutional. Many critics are quick to point out that they are not opposed to religion as such but only to *institutional* religion. Some of them are open to the teachings of the Christian religion, but they react against institutionalizing Christianity. They are willing to say yes to Christ, but they say no to the church.

Ironically, there would be no Christ for us to choose had the church not preached and taught the message of Christ. Every movement, including the Christian religion, must be embodied in some organizational form. If those who have dropped out of the church take seriously what Christians are to be and to do, they will be forced to have some organization. They may not call it a church, but some form is needed to evangelize, educate, worship, and fellowship.

Paul recognized this. When he did his missionary work, he always organized churches. He did not leave his converts to flounder, helpless and alone. Nor did he allow the gospel message to dissipate. He formed churches to strengthen converts and to continue to spread the gospel. The church at Corinth is an example of such a church.

It is, of course, true that institutions do have some inherent weaknesses and potential dangers. The history of Christianity—ancient and modern—is proof enough that churches are imperfect bearers of the eternal gospel. How could it be otherwise since churches are comprised of people?

The early churches had their faults and imperfections just as modern churches do. Surely no one who reads 1 Corinthians can doubt that the Corinthian church was far from perfect. Yet notice how Paul responded to this fact.

He did not give up on the church. To the contrary, he did what he could to help the church be what it should have been. His two letters to the Corinthians are evidence of this fact.

E. Stanley Jones tells of a Japanese girl converted to faith in Christ. She wrote on the back of her decision card: "I am 100% for Christ, but I am only 50% for the church."[2] She was perceptive enough to realize that the church is an imperfect bearer of Christ and his message. To use Paul's analogy, Christ is the matchless treasure, but his followers are only vessels of clay (see 2 Cor. 4:7). Although the percentage of Christ in the church never will be 100 percent, our mission as Christians should be to try to raise the percentage.

Church renewal. One of the encouraging facets of modern Christianity is the interest in church renewal. Writing in the late Sixties, Elton Trueblood noted how much current interest is focused on this issue: "Once, in this century, the great stress was upon foreign missions, while at another time it was on ecumenicity. Neither of these is forgotten, yet neither is at the contemporary center of attention. The present major emphasis of the Church is upon its own renewal."[3]

Trueblood points out that renewal has taken place at other times in history. During the eighteenth century, religion and morality had reached a deplorable state. The churches were cold and formal. Then came the Wesleyan revival. Many Christians are praying that the modern stirrings of church renewal are part of a new spiritual revival of true Christianity.

The church renewal movement takes many forms, but it has these two major premises: (1) *the church needs to be renewed,* and (2) *the church can be renewed.* Those who believe in the need for renewal set themselves apart from some of their fellow-church members who refuse to change or be changed. Church renewal advocates also set themselves apart from the church drop-outs who do not believe the church can be renewed.

Renewal is a new word for many people, at least when it is applied to the church. Some one might ask, "Why not use the more familiar word 'revival'?" Actually, either word could be used to convey the moving of God's Spirit to renew or revive the spiritual life of his people. However, the word "revival," in spite of its noble heritage and rich meaning, has come to have a certain limited connotation. To many people, *revival* means a protracted meeting. *Renewal* has no such connotation. Therefore, it can be used to describe the wide variety of ways in which God's Spirit is breathing new life into his church.

The Bible is the source from which the various approaches to church renewal should be drawn. Church renewal, rightly understood, is not an attempt to change the church into something other than a church. To the contrary, the goal is to renew the church on the basis of biblical teachings.

First Corinthians 11–14 provides a good Bible base for discovering principles relating to church renewal. The word "church" is found more often in 1 Corinthians than in any other book of the New Testament. And over half of the uses of the word in 1 Corinthians are in chapters 11–14. These chapters present various areas of the life of the early church. Paul dealt with three distinct problems: (1) the veiling of women at worship (11:2–16), (2) conduct at the Lord's Supper (11:17–34), and (3) the exercise of spiritual gifts, especially tongue-speaking (12:1 to 14:40).

What Is the Life of The Church? (11:1-34)

Not everything in 1 Corinthians 11–14 relates directly to the modern situation. For example, the first part of chapter 11 deals with a question about women wearing veils in church. Wearing veils in church was considered proper because of the social customs of ancient society. Wearing veils is not an issue today. However, Paul's advice does contain certain principles that relate to the place of women in the church.

Women in the church. Apparently the same spirit was at work in the matter of wearing veils as in the issue of eating meat sacrificed to idols. Some of the Corinthians who considered themselves enlightened were advocating that women appear unveiled at worship services. From a modern point of view, this seems a harmless and even a commendable innovation. However, the custom of the day was for women to wear veils when they went outside their homes. The veil was a sign of modesty and virtue. Only immoral women appeared unveiled in public. This is what Paul had in mind when he said that an unveiled woman might as well have her hair cut off (1 Cor. 11:6). A shaved head was considered a clear sign of an immoral woman.

Therefore, the appearances of unveiled women in the Corinthian church had a disruptive effect on the worship and witness of the church. Paul was willing to allow Christian women to pray and prophesy under certain conditions, and one of these conditions was to remain veiled (v. 5). Later, in 14:34–35, Paul seems to have forbidden women to speak at all in church. However, when these verses are compared with 11:5 and studied in context, it seems that Paul was warning not against speaking at all but against overdoing a good thing. For women to have taken the lead in speaking in church would have violated the rules of social decorum of the day.

Paul also based his objection on what he considered basic principles of human sexuality. One principle is that men and women have distinctive roles that must not be confused. Paul's emphasis here is on the leadership role of the man

(vv. 3, 7–8). However, he did not fail to mention the mutual interdependence of men and women under God: "In the Lord woman is not independent of man nor man of woman; for as woman was made from man, so man is now born of woman. And all things are from God" (vv. 12–13).

Our evaluation of Paul's teachings on this subject should be based on more than this one passage. For example, Ephesians 5:21–33 is his classic exposition of the distinctive yet interdependent roles of men and women. And these principles—especially the teaching about man's leadership role—must be set over against the principle of basic equality in Galatians 3:28: "There is neither Jew nor Greek, there is neither slave nor free, *there is neither male nor female;* for you are all one in Christ Jesus."

Thus Paul might be quoted by either side in the modern debate about women's rights. Actually both sides need to consider the principles set forth by Paul: Men and women are clearly equal in Christ. However, both men and women are needed—each sex with a distinctive yet interdependent role. According to Paul, a person gives glory to God by fulfilling his role—a man being a man and a woman being a woman.

This does not mean that the role of a woman today must conform to the forms of subordination that were part of the social customs of first-century society. In applying biblical teachings, we must distinguish between examples and principles. If this passage were taken literally, women would have to wear veils (not just hats) to church. The abiding principle is that men and women should fulfil their distinctive and interdependent roles to the glory of God.

As far as the role of Christian women in the church is concerned, we must remember that even in New Testament times dedicated Christian women served the Lord through the church. Paul's friend Priscilla is a case in point. Priscilla and her husband Aquila faithfully served the Lord through each of the churches of which they were a part. While they were in Corinth, they worked there; and when they were in Ephesus and Rome, the churches even met in their house. (See Acts 18; Rom. 16:3–4; 1 Cor. 16:19.) Other loyal Christian women include Lydia, whose conversion marked the beginning of the Philippian church (Acts 16:13–15) and Phoebe, a faithful worker in the church of Cenchreae, a suburb of Corinth (see Rom. 16:1–2).

Profaning the Lord's Supper. First Corinthians 11:17–34 is valuable because it contains one of the earliest records of Christian worship. Imbedded in this passage is the earliest biblical record of the institution of the Lord's Supper. (First Corinthians was written before any of the four Gospels.)

In order to understand 1 Corinthians 11:17–34, it is necessary to realize that the Lord's Supper in Corinth was taken in connection with a regular meal. It was not a distinct part of a formal worship service as it is today. The original institution of the Lord's Supper took place in connection with an actual meal Jesus ate with his disciples. The churches in the apostolic era continued this practice. The Lord's Supper was part of a fellowship meal called a "love feast" (see Jude 12). This custom continued until about the fourth century, when it died out, probably as a result of the kinds of abuses reflected in 1 Corinthians 11:17–34.

Verses 17–22 describe the abuses in Corinth. Some members of the church were better off than others. They arrived at the meeting place earlier than the poorer members, who had to work longer hours. The plan called for a sharing of food. Since the poor had less to share, they were dependent on the Christian spirit of their brothers in Christ. However, when the poorer members of the Corinthian church arrived, they found that the others had eaten without them. Perhaps the food was not yet all consumed, but there was no move by the others to share either food or fellowship. As Paul said, "Each one goes ahead with his own meal" (v. 21). The result was that some were well fed and others were hungry.

At some point in the meal, the disciples were supposed to carry out the command of Jesus given at the Last Supper. The Corinthians were probably going through the motions of this, but their actions were a complete denial of the intent and purpose of the Lord's Supper. Therefore, Paul reminded them of the Lord's words when he instituted the Supper (vv. 23–26).

The Lord's Supper is to the Christian what the Passover was to the Israelites. For centuries the Jews have commemorated their deliverance from Egyptian slavery. A faithful Jew seeks to relive the Exodus events when he observes the Passover. In the same way a Christian should recall the divine deliverance from sin effected by the death of Jesus.

But notice that Jesus did not say, "Remember my death"; he said, "Remember *me*." We do recall his death, but not in isolation from his resurrection. He is not a dead sacrifice, but a crucified, risen Lord. The Lord's Supper points in three directions—past, present, and future. Our Lord died and was raised from the dead; he is with us by his Spirit; and he is coming again.

A worshiping fellowship. The Lord's Supper has been the focal point of much modern debate. One school of thought has insisted that Jesus Christ is literally present in the elements of the Lord's Supper. In reaction to this view, others have spent so much time denying the Lord's presence in the elements that they have not affirmed where he is present. Christ is not present in some magical way in the elements of the Lord's Supper, but he is present in the Lord's Supper: he is present in and among his people. In 1 Corinthians 10:16–17 Paul spoke of the Lord's Supper as a communion or participation in the body and blood of Christ shared by the members of the body of Christ.

In many churches the Lord's Supper has become a sterile observance. The infrequency of its observance says something about its lack of deep meaning. The word "sacrament" is unsatisfactory because it implies some kind of saving value in the Lord's Supper itself. On the other hand, the word "symbol" may not say enough about its significance. The Lord's Supper is a sign of the Lord's redemptive work for us and his empowering presence among us. Therefore, it should be a rich experience of worship in which fellow believers share.

The principle of corporate worship involved here extends beyond the specific matter of the Lord's Supper. A life of worship must include both private and corporate worship experiences. Private worship is vital for every Christian, but church worship experiences also are needed. Such shared worship experiences are the life and breath of the church.

This fact is often overlooked by nonchurchgoers—including dropouts and those who have never dropped in. Many people ask, "Why go to church?" They say, "I can worship just as well somewhere else." There is no question about this, but can such private worship take the place of worshiping as a part of God's people?

Why did the Christians in times of Roman persecution meet in the catacombs? They risked their lives to meet with their brothers to worship the Lord. Could they not just as well have gone to some secret place and worshiped alone? This would have been the safe thing to do. No doubt they

did have times of private prayer, but they also came together because of their need for worship and fellowship with
brothers in Christ.

This principle speaks not only to the church dropout but
also to the person interested in church renewal. Unless renewal begins with a shared experience of worship, it is
doomed to fail. Some of those who speak enthusiastically
about the possibilities of church renewal seem to overlook
this fact. One gets the impression that they think of the
church almost solely as a social service agency. This is obviously one area in which many churches need renewal, but
a church that becomes *only* a social service agency ceases
to be a church. A church is essentially a spiritual organism,
and worship is its life and breath.

Elton Trueblood is among those who have advocated
church renewal. He has laid special emphasis on the church
launching out into the world as a witnessing and minister-
ing force. But he has not made this emphasis by slighting
the importance of church worship. Trueblood refers to the
need for the church *gathering* and *scattering*. The church
gathers regularly at its home base for worship, testimonies,
and training. Then it scatters into the world—its field of
witness and service.[4]

Discerning the body. Worship and fellowship belong together because they constitute the life of the church. Fellowship is not something the church promotes; the church *is*
a fellowship—a worshiping fellowship.

The combination of the Lord's Supper with the love feast
was designed to express this fact. The Corinthian church
had made a mockery of both worship and fellowship. Paul
commanded them to avoid taking the Lord's Supper in such
an unworthy way. Otherwise, they became "guilty of profaning the body and blood of the Lord" (v. 27). Paul also
spoke of the danger of not "discerning the body" (v. 29).

Scholars debate the meaning of the words *discerning the body* in verse 29. Some say that Paul was warning against an irreverent failure to remember the Lord's sacrificial death. Others say that the word *body* in verse 29 refers to the church as the body of Christ (see 12:12–27). William Barclay says that Paul's words probably include both meanings.[5] The Corinthians were not only failing to reverently worship the crucified and risen Lord but also failing to recognize the Lord's presence in and among their brothers in Christ.

In 1 Corinthians 1:12–13 Paul had accused them of dismembering the body of Christ by their factions over leaders. They were doing the same thing when they acted selfishly at the love feasts. By disregarding the needs of the poor brothers, they were actually despising the church of God (v. 22).

Paul concluded his discussion of the Lord's Supper by writing: "So then, my brethren, when you come together to eat, wait for one another—if any one is hungry, let him eat at home—lest you come together to be condemned" (vv. 33–34). A superficial reading might seem to indicate that Paul was ordering them not to eat at church. Actually, he was telling them to make the Lord's Supper and love feast a true expression of Christian fellowship and worship.

Since Paul's day, we have separated the Lord's Supper from the fellowship meal. Some experiments in church renewal have attempted to recombine these two New Testament practices. However, even if they remain separate, a church can take seriously the principle involved by seeking ways of expressing its oneness in Christ.

This oneness in Christ is at the heart of the New Testament meaning of the Lord's Supper. This is what should be meant when the Supper is described as a "church ordinance." The Lord's Supper is not a proper occasion for excluding people but an occasion for affirming that Christians take the Supper as brothers in Christ. Of course, the Lord's Supper is meaningless to a non-Christian, but to fellow believers it is an affirmation of their common faith in Christ. Judged in the light of 1 Corinthians 11, "the most serious profaning" of the Lord's Supper "is the manner in which people may come to church and to the Lord's Table as isolated individuals without recognizing or knowing one another, and for practical purposes, devoid even of the most elemental fellowship."[6]

True fellowship, expressed in the Lord's Supper and in other worship experiences, should pervade the entire life of a church. The New Testament word for fellowship refers to a shared life in Christ. This is an inclusive term that includes brothers and sisters in Christ. All kinds of people live in our pluralistic society. God's love in Christ constrains us to try to reach them all with the gospel. That same love demands that we share in the same spiritual family with all of those who commit themselves to Christ.

In India a high-caste Brahman was converted to Christ. This meant complete rejection by his family and friends. This also meant sharing in the Christian fellowship with all kinds of people, including members of the low-caste groups. The new convert endured being rejected by his family and friends. He did this gladly for Christ's sake. Then one day he found himself in church seated next to a low-caste Hindu who was now a Christian brother, and the former Brahman's "stomach turned upside down."[7] Accepting this man as a brother proved to be the hardest test of what he was willing to do for Christ's sake.

What Is the Church? (12:1–31)

A teacher said to one of his students, "You are a gifted boy." Here is the teacher's description of the student's reaction: "He blushed and hardly knew which way to look. He was embarrassed and self-conscious because he had the feeling that I had praised him and ascribed some great quality to him. But of course I was doing no such thing; on the contrary, I was merely saying that he was 'gifted,' which means that his gifts were entrusted to him by someone else. But he too identified himself with them."[8]

The Corinthians made the same mistake. God had given them various gifts to use in his service. However, the Corinthians were acting proudly and selfishly. Each one boasted of his gift as if it were superior to the gifts of others. And he used his gift as if it were his to do with as he pleased.

First Corinthians 12–14 contains Paul's discussion of spiritual gifts. He used two words to describe these gifts. One word, literally meaning "spiritual things," is a form of the word "spirit" (see 12:1). The other word, literally meaning "gift of grace," is the word from which we get our word "charisma." These words emphasize that the gifts come from God's Spirit on the basis of his grace. The proper response to such spiritual gifts is humble gratitude and faithful stewardship.

One body—many members. Paul's main point in chapter 12 is the variety and unity of spiritual gifts. The gifts are of different kinds, but they all come from God's Spirit (see vv. 1–11). The words "for the common good" in verse 7 set the tone not only for chapter 12 but also for the entire discussion of spiritual gifts in chapters 12–14: The intended purpose of each spiritual gift is to help build up the whole body of believers, not just some individual possessor of the gift.

Paul's most forceful illustration of this truth is his description of the church as the body of Christ: "For just as the body is one and has many members, and all the members of the body, though many, are one body, so it is with Christ. For by one Spirit we were all baptized into one body—Jews or Greeks, slaves or free—and all were made to drink of one Spirit" (vv. 12–13).

Producers of church literature are always anxious to receive evaluations of their materials by those who use the materials. All of the feedback is helpful to some degree, but some is less helpful than others. In the latter category was the suggestion from one user of materials produced by the Sunday School Board: "Why all this talk about the body of Christ in our literature? Why not spend more time describing what the church really is?"

One hardly knows how to respond to such a suggestion. After all, was "the body of Christ" not one of Paul's most popular analogies to describe the church? (See Rom. 12:4–5; Eph. 1:22–23; 4:15–16; Col. 2:10.) Of course, it is only an analogy; but if this analogy does not illustrate *what the church really is,* what does? What better way to describe the relationship between Christ and his people? What better way to describe the tie that binds together fellow believers?

This also is an ideal analogy to use in explaining the proper use of spiritual gifts. Paul made the most of it. In the background were those who were boasting of their superior gifts; others felt a resulting mixture of frustration, envy, and inferiority. Paul hammered away at this problem by stressing that "the body does not consist of one member but of many" (v. 14). He made this point in several ways:

1. *Each member is important* (vv. 15–16).—No part of the body should feel excluded because it is not a more prominent part. The foot should not feel unimportant because it is not a hand; nor an ear, because it is not an eye.

2. *No one member is the entire body* (vv. 17–20).—The body is one, but there are many parts. And no one part is

the whole body. An eye is very important, but an eye cannot hear or perform other needed functions of the body.

3. *The members are mutually dependent on one another* (vv. 21–24).—No part can get along without the others: "The eye cannot say to the hand, 'I have no need of you,' nor again the head to the feet, 'I have no need of you' " (v. 21). This principle applies not only to the more prominent parts of the body, but also to the seemingly insignificant parts.

Christian togetherness. The application of this analogy to the life of the church should be obvious. But lest anyone miss the point, Paul spelled it out: "God has so adjusted the body . . . that there may be no discord in the body, but that the members may have the same care for one another. If one member suffers, all suffer together; if one member is honored, all rejoice together" (vv. 24–26).

This is a beautiful expression of the inner life of the church. The Greek word is *koinōnia*. This word is translated in various ways—"fellowship," "participation," "communion." It describes that which is shared or held in common. The word is used in 10:16–17 to describe the shared experience of the church as one body partaking of the Lord's Supper. The word itself is not used in chapter 12, but the body of Christ analogy perfectly demonstrates what *koinōnia* is. It is more than just cooperating together; it is sharing together in the same common life in Christ.

The members of the body of Christ care for one another; they suffer and rejoice together. The members are bound together in such a way that what affects one affects all the others. The suffering of one part of the human body affects all the parts; so it should be in the church. Likewise the joy and health of part of the body is shared by all. Human nature being what it is, we sometimes find it easier to weep with those who are weeping than to rejoice with those who are rejoicing. Often we are more envious than glad for the good fortune of a brother. But since he is a fellow member of Christ's body, we should rejoice because his good fortune belongs to the entire body.

Any successful attempt to renew the church must reproduce something of this spirit of *koinōnia*. This Christian togetherness must go deeper than any superficial camaraderie. Christians must genuinely care for one another and share with one another at the deepest levels of life—bearing one another's burdens, praying for one another, and confessing their faults to one another.

Such deep sharing takes place best in small groups. Churches of all sizes—large and small—are becoming increasingly aware of the value of small groups within the church. The entire church can express its oneness in many ways, but Christian togetherness on a deep, personal level requires small groups. Churches need to share at both levels—in the larger scope of the entire church and in the more intimate participation of a small group. Both are needed. The person who shares only in the public worship services of his church misses sharing at a deeper level. The person who shares only in the small group loses a sense of identity with the total life and mission of the church.

In an attempt at renewal, many small groups have sprung up outside the structure of the church's organized small groups. Such groups have often been instrumental in revitalizing a spirit of Christian togetherness for those who share in them. However, the real challenge for most churches is to cultivate a spirit of *koinōnia* in the existing small groups of its organizations.

A Sunday School class, for example, should be more than a group that meets each week to hear a Bible lesson taught. It should be a caring and sharing fellowship where Paul's words in verses 25–26 are literally applied. Such a group does not major on learning facts about the Bible by listening to someone talk. It majors on finding answers to life's questions and problems by searching the Scriptures together. In order for this to take place, the teacher and members must be willing to share with one another at life's deepest levels—balancing openness and honesty with kindness and compassion.

Spectators or participants? In chapter 12 Paul made two lists of spiritual gifts—in verses 8–10 and in verse 28. The rich variety illustrates the many different ways in which God's Spirit equips his people for service.

The most obvious misapplication of this teaching is a rigid distinction between clergy and laity. For all practical purposes, many churches have lumped all these gifts together and assigned them as part of the job description of an ordained minister. According to this view, the job of the laymen is to provide financial support so that the minister can function.

One of the signs of hope for renewal is a new emphasis on lay involvement in the life and work of the church. This new lay movement is recapturing the true spirit of 1 Corinthians and the New Testament as a whole. The church is the body of Christ. No one man—minister or otherwise—is the whole body. Little wonder that the body often functions so poorly when only one or a few are expected to be the whole body. The ministry of the body of Christ is the ministry of *all* its members. The pastor has a leading role in this; his job is to equip the saints for the work of the ministry (see Eph. 4:11–13). All the members of the body of Christ share in this ministry, each performing the gift assigned to him by the Lord.

This requires that members be participants in the life of the church. Elton Trueblood has referred to churchgoing as "America's biggest spectator sport." His point is all too true: Many church members are only spectators at a church worship service. They are not involved either in the worship experience of the church or in the vital service and ministry that should result from that worship experience. If a church's life is to be renewed, something must be done to break this lifeless pattern.

When Is a Church Successful? (13:1–13)

First Corinthians 13 is among the most famous chapters in the Bible. The poetic beauty of its words is surpassed only by the inspiring challenge of its message. Some scholars believe that Paul had composed this hymnlike description of Christian love as a separate work; then he inserted it at this point in his letter to the Corinthians. Paul may have said something like this on more than one occasion, but the chapter as it now stands is an integral part of 1 Corinthians. Although it is often read as a unit in itself, the chapter is most meaningful when it is studied—as it was written—as a part of 1 Corinthians directly related to chapters 12—14.

The message of Christian love made explicit in chapter 13 is one of the main themes of the letter. The "wisdom of the cross" described in chapter 1 is set over against the selfish pride and strife called the "wisdom of the world." The word "love" is not used in chapter 1, but the idea is clearly the same. The word itself appears in Paul's description of the problem of meat sacrificed to idols. Again the solution was not worldly knowledge and wisdom but Christian love (see 8:1, 3).

The same basic problem appeared in the matter of spiritual gifts, and once again Paul challenged the Corinthians to rely on love instead of worldly wisdom. In chapter 12 Paul discussed some basic principles in using spiritual gifts. Verse 31 is a key verse that contains two important principles: First of all, Paul said, "Earnestly desire the higher gifts." (Judging from Paul's two lists of gifts in 12:8–10, 27–30, "higher gifts" refers to such things as preaching and teaching. In each list, "tongues" is placed last. Later, chapter 14 elaborates on this point.) Secondly, Paul said, "I will show you a still more excellent way." Chapter 13 describes this "more excellent way," which should govern the use of any and all spiritual gifts.

What is love? The key word in chapter 13 is the Greek word *agapē*. The English language has no word that captures the meaning of *agapē*. The translators of the King James Version used the word "charity." But what we mean today by charity and what Paul meant by *agapē* are two different things. Verse 3 in the King James Version reads: "Though I bestow all my goods to feed the poor . . . and have not *charity, it* profiteth me nothing." To us, bestowing our goods to feed the poor *is* charity.

Most English translations contain the word "love." But few words in any language are more ambiguous. Think of the contrasting ways the word "love" is used today. Imagine that you are an immigrant trying to learn the English language. What would you conclude is the meaning of *love?* You would often hear the word equated with romantic love and sexual attraction. You would also hear the same word used of love for other people—family, friends, even humanity as a whole. Then in church, you would hear the preacher talk about the love of God. How confusing!

Therefore, in explaining the meaning of Christian love, the teacher must do what the translator cannot do—interpret the distinctive meaning of *agapē*. The Greek language is rich in words that describe various facets of love. For example, one word describes erotic love and another describes brotherly love. The word *agapē* is yet another word which emphasizes concern for others. The New Testament writers used this word as a vehicle for the distinctive message of Christian love.

By the New Testament definition, God himself is *agapē* (1 John 4:8). God showed his self-giving concern for sinful men by the sending of his Son (John 3:16). The death of Christ is the supreme demonstration of divine *agapē* (Rom. 5:8). Christian love for God and others is the result of experiencing God's love in Christ (2 Cor. 5:14).

Paul did not try to define *agapē* in chapter 13; instead he described how it works: "Love is patient and kind; love is not jealous or boastful; it is not arrogant or rude. Love does not insist on its own way; it is not irritable or resent-ful; it does not rejoice at wrong, but rejoices in the right. Love bears all things, believes all things, hopes all things, endures all things" (vv. 4–7).

Christian love is the opposite way of life to that way lived by men without God. This world's way treats others as victims, rivals, or nothings. In each case the emphasis is on selfish attainment: Victims are those from whom something is taken. Rivals stir up feelings of pride when we have something they don't and feelings of envy when they have something we want. "Nothings" can usually be ignored unless they get in our way and become either victims or rivals.

By contrast, Christian love focuses on others as persons. Like divine *agapē,* it is self-giving. It acts on behalf of others, regardless of their merit or lack of merit. Christian love enters into relationships with others not for what can be gained but for what can be given.

The Pilgrims' first winter at Plymouth was a disastrous one. Disease raged for weeks, and more than half of the colonists died. Disease also raged aboard the *Mayflower* anchored in the harbor. Some of the Pilgrims were on board with the sailors. The crew of the *Mayflower* had ridiculed and cursed the Pilgrims all during the long trans-Atlantic voyage. Now when many of the sailors lay sick, the crew saw how Christian love responds to such treatment. The healthy members of the crew would not go near their own sick, but the Pilgrims cared for the sick sailors just as they did for their own.[9]

The Pilgrims could have taken a self-righteous attitude and said: "They're only getting what they deserve." Or they could have ignored them and justified themselves by saying: "Let their own friends help them; we've got our own sick to tend to. Besides, why should we help those who mistreated us?" However, they chose instead to act in the true spirit of Christian *agapē*.

The measure of Christian "success." The Corinthians were measuring their success in terms of the possession of certain spiritual gifts. According to Paul, the true measure was the degree of Christian *agapē*. The value of all spiritual gifts—not only tongues but also teaching and preaching—is limited to the present age; but love is eternal. When tongues have ceased and knowledge has passed away, love will remain (see vv. 8–13).

Verses 1–3 are powerful and pointed: Love is absolutely indispensable; everything minus love equals nothing. Without love, the most ecstatic tongue speaking and the most inspired preaching are just so much noise. Without love, special insight into the greatest divine mysteries and extraordinary miracle-working power are nothing. Even if a person gave away all he possessed and gave up his own life as a martyr, he would gain nothing if he did not act in love.

This is a forceful way of saying that everything a church or Christian does must be measured by Christian love. Therefore, 1 Corinthians 13 provides an instrument by which we may measure our success by God's standards. God's standards often are completely contrary to worldly standards of success. Unfortunately, our goals are often more strongly influenced by human rather than divine standards of success.

When the disciples of Jesus were arguing about which of them would be the greatest, Jesus warned them against adopting such worldly standards as position and power. He taught that true greatness is measured in terms of self-giving service to others (Mark 10:35–45; Luke 22:24–27). In a similar situation, Paul was trying to teach the same lesson to the Corinthian church.

Churches and Christians live in this tension between divine and human measures of success. In this, we are strongly influenced by how society measures success. Statistical measures of success are often given more weight than such intangibles as patience, kindness, humility, and forgiveness. No way has yet been found for a church to include these items in its annual report. Therefore, such factors as members, budgets, and buildings often become the main criteria of a church's success.

Judged by these superficial factors, "a successful church . . . is one that meets in an adequate building, whose statistics are greater this year than they were the year before, that is acceptable in the community whatever the cost of that may be, that fits into the culture which it represents, and is accounted more successful if its constituency is composed of the erudite, the educated, and the wealthy."[10]

This is hardly an adequate measure of success. Judged by the standard of Christian love, such a "successful" church might be an abysmal failure. Of course, this does not mean that statistical success is the antithesis of Christian love. But it does mean that real success must be measured by New Testament standards, not by the standards of modern society.

When Is a Church Spiritual? (14:1–40)

Keep in mind that the problem throughout chapters 12–14 has to do with spiritual gifts, especially the misuse of tongues. The Corinthians prized the idea of being spiritual, and some of them considered tongues the apex of spirituality. In dealing with problems in earlier chapters, Paul showed that his definition of spirituality differed from theirs (see 3:1–4). The same difference is apparent in regard to speaking in tongues.

The problem of tongues is in the background in chapters 12 and 13 (see 12:10, 28, 30; 13:1, 8), but it is in the foreground in chapter 14. Paul had already set forth two basic principles for the use of spiritual gifts: (1) seek the higher gifts and (2) practice Christian *agapē* in the use of any gifts. In chapter 14, the apostle applied these two principles to the question of speaking in tongues.

Speaking in tongues. Verses 1–5 set the tone for chapter 14. Paul made it plain that the person who acts in Christian love will consider prophesying (preaching) a higher gift than tongue speaking. The person who speaks in tongues engages in a private devotional exercise in which he alone is benefited. But the person who speaks a clear message of testimony helps others. Therefore, tongues is a valid gift, but as far as the church is concerned, it is much less important than speaking in order to communicate. Engaging in a private devotional exercise at a public worship service is a selfish act that denies the heart of Christian *agapē*—acting in such a way as to help others.

Verses 6–12 identify what Paul meant by the gift of tongues—unintelligible sounds, comparable to instrumental music or a foreign language. This sets tongue-speaking in Corinth apart from the unique miracle of Pentecost, when men heard the gospel in their own languages. The miracle of speaking and/or hearing recorded in Acts 2 resulted in a clear communication of the gospel. By contrast, the tongues at Corinth could not be understood by the hearers.

In this sense it was apparently comparable to the modern phenomena of tongue-speaking. Scattered occurrences of tongues have taken place at many stages of Christian history. However, speaking in tongues has really come into its own during this century. The Pentecostal movement has given tongue-speaking a prominent place in their beliefs and practices. More recently, speaking in tongues has become more common even among non-Pentecostal groups.

Proponents of this movement point to tongues as a key to church renewal. They make great claims for the value of tongues as a means of revitalizing spiritual life in general. Those who do not speak in tongues are often willing to acknowledge that tongues is a valid gift, but they insist that 1 Corinthians 14 be the guideline for its use. This chapter is the only New Testament statement about the proper use of tongues; therefore it should be taken seriously.

Some of those who speak in tongues are careful to follow Paul's guidelines, but others are not. In the latter case, the result is often a reoccurrence of the problems at Corinth: tongue-speaking then becomes an expression of pride and an occasion for division in the church. Sometimes, tongues is presented as the only explicit evidence for the fulness of the Spirit, therefore something to be sought diligently by all Christians. This teaching is not consistent with the New Testament; in fact, it contradicts what Paul taught—that tongues is a far less important gift than other gifts and that the higher gifts, not tongues, are to be earnestly sought. Paul's words in verses 13–19 cannot be ignored, especially verse 19. Advocates of tongue-speaking often quote verse 18, but fail to mention verse 19.[11] In verse 18, Paul wrote, "I thank God that I speak in tongues more than you all." But in verse 19 he made his real point: "Nevertheless, in church I would rather speak five words with my mind, in order to instruct others than ten thousand words in a tongue."

Could anything be more devastating to an overemphasis on tongues? As Frank Stagg points out in a study of tongue-speaking in the New Testament, Paul's preference in verse 19 was two thousand to one! Stagg goes on to comment on verse 18: "When Paul said that he spoke in tongues more than others (14:18), he was following his familiar pattern of meeting opponents on their own ground. For example, in refuting Judaizers, he pointed out that he had a better record than they in keeping the Law (Phil. 3:1–11). If the Corinthians could boast of speaking in tongues, so could he. But he did not boast!"[12]

Tests of spirituality. In dealing with the problem of tongues, Paul set forth two tests that measure the value of a spiritual gift. One of the tests, set forth in verses 1–19, raises this question: To what degree does the exercise of this spiritual gift contribute to the moral and spiritual life of others in the church? The second test, set forth in verses 20–25, raises another important question: To what degree does the exercise of this spiritual gift clearly communicate the gospel to non-Christians?

Paul admitted that there is a sense in which tongues is a "sign . . . for unbelievers" (v. 22), but he apparently considered it only a sign of judgment on a fixed attitude of unbelief. Tongues is of no positive value in communicating the gospel to outsiders; to the contrary, Paul says: "If . . . the whole church assembles and all speak in tongues, and outsiders or unbelievers enter, will they not say that you are mad? But if all prophesy, and an unbeliever or outsider enters, he is convicted by all, he is called to account by all, the secrets of his heart are disclosed; and so, falling on his face, he will worship God and declare that God is really among you" (vv. 23–25).

These two tests—helping other Christians and communicating the gospel to outsiders—apply to more than the question of tongues. These are valid tests for every area of a church's life. True spirituality is that which contributes most to mutual upbuilding of church members and results in a clear witness to unbelievers. These two areas are indispensable for any attempt at church renewal on biblical principles.

Take, for example, the matter of contributing to the upbuilding of fellow church members. Too many members think of their church only in terms of personal benefit, not as a channel of service to others. Their commitment seldom gets beyond the circle of their own personal concerns. *Convenience*, not *commitment*, is their byword. They attend, give, and serve only if it is convenient to them.

This lack of commitment may be the biggest challenge to efforts at church renewal. Something must be done to make church membership an expression of sincere, intelligent, and meaningful Christian commitment. Such efforts may be directed at three levels of church life:

1. Those who enter the church must do so on the basis of nothing less than a genuine initial commitment to Christ as personal Lord and Savior.

2. Those within the church must be involved not only in a disciplined life of personal spiritual growth but also in active participation in deeds of Christian love and service.

3. Those members who continue to show no evidences of Christian commitment should be considered as outsiders,

and thus as persons who need to be won to an initial commitment to Christ as Lord and Savior.

The second test of spirituality—communicating the gospel to unbelievers—also demands priority. Efforts at church renewal run the risk of becoming preoccupied with the internal affairs of the church. A purely inward concern, however genuine, will eventually stagnate. Therefore, a church must lift up its eyes, look on the fields ripe unto harvest and make every effort to win the lost. In actual practice there is no conflict between these two tests of spirituality. Strange as it seems, the church that loses itself in witness and ministry to the outside world is also the church that finds renewed spiritual fervor and inner warmth of fellowship.

E. Stanley Jones gives this illustration of the priority of Christian witnessing: "When the Constitution of India was being debated, the question of 'the right to profess, practice and propagate one's faith is guaranteed' was up. Many Hindus gagged over 'propagate.' But a Hindu arose and said, 'To propagate one's faith is an integral part of the Christian's faith, so if you do not give the Christians the right to propagate you do not give them the right to profess and practice, for they cannot profess and practice if they do not propagate.' "[13] As Dr. Jones goes on to point out, this Hindu showed more insight into the true nature of Christian faith than many Christians do. The very nature of our faith demands that we make every effort to communicate the gospel to the world.

Channeling spiritual power. The theme of 1 Corinthians 14:26–40 is that "all things should be done decently and in order" (v. 40). Paul laid down some guidelines about conducting a church worship service. He allowed only two or three persons to speak in tongues, and he insisted that each of these must have someone to interpret the meaning of his experience. Paul even placed a limit of the number of prophets who should speak, and he said that they should speak one at a time.

An important principle is involved here: a church needs a proper balance between freedom and order. The need in Corinth was for more order. Their unbridled expressions of spiritual fervor were damaging the church's inner life and outward witness. Actually, freedom and order are both important. Paul wanted to allow every opportunity for the expression of genuine spiritual fervor, but he wanted this zeal to be channeled, not wasted nor misused. So he called for more emphasis on order in Corinth.

Many modern churches are too heavily weighted in the opposite direction: order has become so stilted and rigid that freedom is almost nonexistent. Worship services are so cut and dried that everything is completely predictable and totally unexciting. (The current interest in speaking in tongues may be interpreted as a reaction against the stiff formality of much contemporary religion.) If renewal is to take place in many churches, there must be more opportunities for dynamic participation and spontaneous sharing.

Every church lives in the tension between the church as an institution and the church as a community of the Spirit. The church is a community of the Spirit, but it must function in some institutional form. The body of Christ is a living organism, but it is embodied in organizational forms. However, care should be taken to see that the organization is such that the vitality of the organism can find full expression. Otherwise, the church may fall into the snare of institutionalism.

Institutionalism takes place when the organization becomes an end in itself. As Findley B. Edge says: "Religion becomes institutionalized when its adherents are related primarily to the church as an institution or to the organizations of the church rather than to the living God. The religious life manifested is not the free and open outworking of a deep, spiritual relationship with God. Rather, in institutionalized religion the primary expression of a person's religion is that he supports the organizations by his attendance; he supports the institution by his gifts; and in general he merely lives a 'good' life."[14]

Viewed from this perspective, the current wave of criticisms directed against institutional religion is understandable. Much of the criticism is justified: the pitfalls of institutionalism are real; many churches have fallen into some or all of these.

One thing seems certain: support of the church as an institution is declining. In other days, it was not uncommon for a high degree of loyalty toward institutional religion to be demonstrated. People attended, gave, and worked in order to support their church. Today there is much less support for the church as an organization. Much still exists; but it is declining, particularly among the young, who are the generation of the future. The obvious conclusion is that fewer people in the future will support the church for its own sake.

This can either frighten or challenge those of us who still believe in the church. If we spend our time wringing our hands in dismay, a great opportunity will pass us by. On the other hand, if we pray and work for renewal of the church, we will find that many of the harshest critics of institutional religion will be forced to acknowledge the continuing work of God's Spirit in and through his people. When an unbeliever or outsider comes into contact with a spiritually renewed church, "he is convicted by all, he is called to account by all, the secrets of his heart are disclosed; and so, falling on his face, he will worship God and declare that God is really among you" (1 Cor. 14:24-25)

6 The Sting of Death

The French sculptor Rodin has tried to imagine how mankind first responded to the awful mystery of death. His work, called "The First Funeral," depicts Adam and Eve looking at the dead body of Abel. Their emotions are reflected in their facial expressions: Eve is distracted with grief; Adam looks down in sorrow and bewilderment at the cold, limp form in his arms.

Since mankind's first experience with death, an inevitable question has been, "What about death?" The question is somewhat academic until a person must actually cope with the death of a loved one or until he must go through the experience of his own dying. Then the question becomes personal and real.

Elisabeth Kübler-Ross tells of an eight-year-old boy who was dying from an inoperable brain tumor. The child expressed his feelings about dying in the pictures he drew. One picture in particular showed his feeling of helplessness. In the background of his picture were a house, sunshine, trees, and grass. In the foreground he drew an army tank. In front of the barrel of the tank was a tiny figure with a stop sign in his hand.

This helplessness is what makes death so frightening. Dr. Ross compares the fear of death to an iceburg. Our conscious fears of death are like the visible part of the iceburg—we fear suffering, being a burden to others, and being separated from loved ones. The unconscious fear of death is like the hidden part of the iceberg—the fear of an overwhelming force before which we are completely helpless. Like the tiny figure with the stop sign, we cannot halt the tank.

A death-denying society. Dr. Ross made these observations in a lecture on "Death in a Death-Denying Society" given at Johns Hopkins University. She spoke out of her experience in working with dying patients. Dr. Ross, along with many others, is convinced that ours is a death-denying society. And she is equally convinced that the refusal to face the reality of death makes many Americans unable either to cope with their own dying or to help others who are dying.[1]

Modern American society has tried to banish death by refusing to face the reality of death. Many Americans try to create what Peter Marshall called "the illusion of mortal immortality":

We will not face reality.
We are all trying desperately to keep up a pretense.
We are pretending that we are not getting any older—that we are not afraid of death.
We are all busy in a vain effort to create the illusion of mortal immortality.
Age creeps on, but we refuse to recognize it.
We enlist the help of the masseuse and the golf pro
    the dressmaker and the tailor
   creams and lotions
  hair dyes and plastic surgeons
all in an effort to keep alive the illusion that life here will go on forever."[2]

The fact of death itself should shatter this illusion. Every day more than five thousand Americans die. But American culture has built-in insulators against facing the reality of death and dying. The elderly are isolated in "Sunset Villages" and the dying are moved to hospitals. Four out of five people die in hospitals. The very agencies for preserving and prolonging life also insulate people against facing death's reality. Terminal patients often are not told that they are dying. Family members often are not present when loved ones die—at least, not actually with them. Often the only ones who have direct contact with death are the professionals most accustomed to dealing with it.

In less sophisticated times, a person died at home with his family very much aware of his dying. Children grew up accepting death as a normal and natural part of life. By contrast, many children today are shielded against death, even the mention of it.

The result is a conspiracy of silence about death in American society. Death is probably the only unmentionable subject left in our outspoken times. The word "death" sticks in our throats. Even in the presence of death, people talk about a person "passing on," not "dying".

Funeral customs have helped support this kind of make-believe. The modern mortician's skill is judged by how lifelike he can make the dead body appear. The minister is expected to speak briefly and to avoid any unpleasant reminder that the dead person is actually dead.

No wonder many people have difficulty coping with death and dying. All of our training and experience have conditioned us to deny death.

A group of housewives were enlisted to aid in hospital visitation. They were told that some of the patients were dying. The housewives stated a willingness to visit all the patients, but in actual practice they concentrated on the merely sick and avoided direct or prolonged involvement with those who were dying. They used various evasions, perhaps unconsciously, to avoid confronting the fearful reality of death. At a time when many terminal patients desperately need to talk with someone, these women refused to care enough to expose themselves to such a painful experience.

A death-defying society. This tendency to *deny* death has been contrasted with an outlook that enabled earlier generations to *defy* death. Earlier generations were sometimes overly morbid, and they were sometimes too preoccupied with the next world. However, their basic Christian outlook produced a more healthy philosophy of life and death than the modern stance: "Death could be faced; it could be talked about with friends and neighbors; it could be treated as normal and as a natural end. For the conviction that all was in the hands and will of God made it possible to gaze at the end of life with hope. Meaning and fulfilment in life and in death were possible within the bounds of a personal relation to God."[3]

Unfortunately, modern American society has no real confidence in the Christian hope. Earlier generations could *affirm* death precisely because they could *defy* death. Our culture is almost forced to deny death because it has lost its faith in the life-giving power of God. Many people today have been educated in a totally secular climate, which begins with the assumption that the Christian hope of eternal life is impossible and incredible.

Although our society sometimes still gives lip service to the Christian symbols of life and hope, there is an underlying feeling of skepticism and despair. The minister conducting a funeral is expected to read such words of hope and assurance as those spoken by Jesus in John 11:25–26. But the attitude of the hearers often seems to be: "I don't really believe what he is saying. I would like to, but I can't. But it can't do any harm for such words to be said. Maybe it might even do some good, but I doubt it."

What of those Americans who profess to believe in life after death? Many of them believe in some form of immortality of the soul, not resurrection of the body. Many Christians state their hope in terms of the survival of some inher-

ently eternal part of them rather than in terms of the trans-
forming and life-giving power of God. The former view has
much in common with some forms of ancient Greek philosophy and religion; the latter is the biblical view. The classic
explanation of the biblical view is in 1 Corinthians 15.

One of the obvious parallels between the situations in ancient Corinth and in modern America is in attitudes toward
death. The Greeks held one of two views about death:
many of them were in utter despair about death; others, influenced by Plato's philosophy and/or the mystery religions,
held to a view of soul immortality. According to this latter
view, the soul is inherently immortal. During life the soul
is imprisoned in the body, but death liberates the soul.
Some of the Greeks also taught the preexistence of the soul
and the reincarnation of the soul.

What was the problem at Corinth? Paul referred to those
in the Corinthian church who said that "there is no resurrection of the dead" (1 Cor. 15:12). It is not certain
whether these Corinthians denied all kinds of life after
death or whether they only denied resurrection while affirming immortality. In either case, they denied the future resurrection. In 2 Timothy 2:16–18 Paul warned against some
false teachers who "swerved from the truth by holding that
the resurrection is past already." Perhaps the Corinthian
Christians stressed the past spiritual resurrection of believers (see John 5:24) but denied their future resurrection.

Probably the situation in Corinth was too complex for
any one explanation. The views toward death of the cosmopolitan Corinthians probably varied. Many Corinthians,
certainly those outside the church, had no hope of any kind
in the face of death. Others believed in immortality of the
soul but not in resurrection of the body.

Over against these views, Paul set forth the Christian
hope of the future resurrection of believers based on the

resurrection of Jesus Christ from the dead. The despair and false hopes of our day need to be challenged by these basic affirmations of Christian hope.

If Christ Be Not Risen (15:1-19)

In recent years the Christian religion has sometimes been watered down to little more than some general guidelines for proper conduct. Although Christianity is a way of life, morality is not the focal point of Christian faith. Christian living is the *fruit,* not the *root.* The apostles of Christ did not turn the ancient world upside down by proclaiming ethics. Rather they proclaimed the good news of Christ's victory over sin and death.

The resurrection of Jesus Christ. Paul began his discussion of the problem of death by reminding the Corinthians of this redeeming gospel: "For I delivered to you as of first importance what I also received, that Christ died for our sins in accordance with the scriptures, that he was buried, that he was raised on the third day in accordance with the scriptures" (vv. 3–4).

The tense of the word translated "was raised" is different from the tense of the words "died" and "buried." The word describing Christ's resurrection is in the perfect tense, which "suggests both that the raising happened, and that it remains in force. Christ died, but he is not dead; he was buried, but he is not in the grave; he was raised, and he is alive now."[4]

Paul then spelled out the historical basis for his witness to the risen Lord. He mentioned the appearances of Christ to Cephas (v. 5), to the twelve (v. 5), to more than five hundred brothers (v. 6), to James (v. 7), to all the apostles (v. 7), and finally to Paul himself (vv. 8–11). Paul wrote to the Corinthians several years before the four Gospels were written. Thus 1 Corinthians 15:1–11 contains the earliest written New Testament record of the appearances of the risen Lord.

Paul, like the Gospel writers, based his witness to the resurrection of Christ on the appearances of the Lord. The Christian faith is not based on wishful thinking but on the fact that God raised Jesus Christ from the dead. Although Jesus had predicted his death and resurrection, the disciples were taken by surprise by both events. The crucifixion overwhelmed them with despair, showing that Jesus' previous predictions had fallen on deaf ears. The disciples certainly were not expecting his resurrection. In fact, when it happened, they had to be convinced (see Luke 24:11; John 20:24–25). Only when they saw him alive were they convinced.

Paul preached the gospel of the cross and the resurrection in spite of the fact that both ideas were stumbling-blocks to many of his hearers. The message of Christ crucified seemed weak and foolish to the cultured people of the Greco-Roman world (1 Cor. 1:21–24). Likewise, the message of the resurrection seemed incredible. Paul received laughter and ridicule when he tried to proclaim the resurrection to the philosophers in Athens (Acts 17:31–32).

Since Paul's day, many people have stumbled at the proclamation of Christ's resurrection. Many skeptics have proposed ingenious theories to explain it away. Over the years some skeptics have adopted the theory that the disciples stole the body of Christ (see Matt. 28:13). Then the disciples are supposed to have gone forth to live and die for a colossal hoax. This theory is much more incredible than the resurrection miracle itself!

One of the most ingenious theories has been set forth by Hugh J. Schonfield in his book *The Passover Plot.*[5] This is a novel form of the old "hallucination" theory, which assumes that the disciples saw someone or something that they thought was Jesus raised from the dead. Schonfield believes that a few close friends, including Joseph of Arimathea, plotted with Jesus to drug him while he was on the cross and later to revive him in the tomb. Then Jesus could appear as if risen from the dead. Unfortunately, Jesus suffered mortal wounds. He did not die on the cross, but he died in the tomb surrounded by his fellow conspirators. As he died, Jesus asked one of these men to carry on his work. After he died, the friends took his body and secretly buried it.

The disciples themselves knew nothing of this. Therefore, they were genuinely surprised by the empty tomb, which suggested to them the possibility of Jesus' resurrection. The man whom Jesus had asked to continue his work was in the garden when Mary Magdalene came. Mary saw him and mistook him for Jesus. All the later appearances of Jesus are explained by Schonfield as instances of the disciples seeing this same man or someone like him. Presumably, the disciples were so anxious to believe that they jumped to the conclusion that Jesus had been raised from the dead.

Schonfield begins with two basic assumptions: (1) the resurrection could not have happened; and (2) the New Testament records are not reliable. He stresses that the Gospels were written a generation after the events described by men who were prejudiced in favor of the view that Jesus had been raised from the dead. But Schonfield would have us believe that his own prejudiced account, nineteen centuries removed from the actual events, can accurately construct what actually happened, using the supposedly distorted New Testament documents as his primary sources. This takes real credulity!

Schonfield plays fast and loose with his primary sources at several points: (1) There is absolutely no New Testament evidence of any so-called "Passover Plot." (2) There is no doubt that Jesus died on the cross. His enemies and the

Roman officials were careful to make sure that he was actually dead (Mark 15:42–45; John 19:31–37). (3) The most flagrant distortion concerns the appearances of Jesus to his disciples. The disciples were in no mood to jump to any conclusion about Jesus' resurrection. They were not expecting it, and when it happened they did not believe until they were convinced by evidence. The disciples knew Jesus well enough not to mistake someone else for him. His appearances and his words to them were unmistakably those of Jesus.

The basis of Christian hope. Paul reminded the Corinthians in verses 1-11 that they had been saved by a gospel of which the resurrection of Christ was a central fact. Then he asked, "Now if Christ is preached as raised from the dead, how can some of you say that there is no resurrection of the dead" (v. 12). Apparently the Corinthians had not questioned the resurrection of Christ. To the contrary, they accepted this as a part of their faith. What they questioned was the future resurrection of believers.

Therefore, Paul drove home his point: "But if there is no resurrection of the dead, then Christ has not been raised" (v. 13). In other words, Paul insisted that the resurrection of Christ and the resurrection of believers stand or fall together; to deny one is to deny the other. Paul showed the Corinthians that they held an untenable position. Their denial of the future resurrection was an implicit denial of the resurrection of Christ. And this denial would undercut the whole basis of the Christian life, message, and hope.

Verses 12-19 are powerful because Paul boldly spelled out the depressing situation that would exist if Christ was not raised from the dead. The resurrection is the foundation on which everything else is built. If the foundation is weak, the entire structure collapses.

"If Christ has not been raised, then our preaching is in

vain. . . . We are even found to be misrepresenting God" (vv. 14–15). The Christian gospel is based on the resurrection of Jesus Christ from the dead. If he was not raised, Christian preaching is not only empty but false.

"If Christ has not been raised, your faith is futile and you are still in your sins" (v. 17). Those who believed the Christian gospel of resurrection have been deceived if this gospel is false. We believed we were saved from sin, and we set out to live a new life on the basis of this gospel. But this is all a delusion if the resurrection did not take place.

Paul spelled out another depressing possibility if Christ has not been raised, "Then those also who have fallen asleep in Christ have perished" (v. 18). All the words of hope spoken at the graves of the dead in Christ are empty and false if Christ is not alive. Job had asked, "If a man die, shall he live again?" (Job 14:14). Christians answer with a triumphant "Yes." But if Christ was not raised, the answer must be "No."

Verse 19 has been translated and interpreted in two different ways. The Revised Standard Version (1959, edition) presents one possibility, "If for *this life only* we have hoped in Christ, we are of all men most to be pitied." This translation assumes that the word "only" qualifies the words "in this life." The point would be that Christians are to be pitied if their only hope is an earthly hope, not an eternal hope.

This is a possible meaning, but the more probable translation sees the word "only" as referring to the word "hoped": "If we have *only hoped* in Christ in this life, we are of all men most pitiable" (American Standard Version). "If Christ be not risen, there is no real basis for Christian hope; believers have only hoped as unbelievers hope—with no foundation for their hopes."[6] James Moffatt observes: "It is as though Paul had said, 'hope set on Christ—and nothing more than hope! Is that all, a mere wistful, faint trust in some larger hope, which rests on nothing?' "[7]

Such a prospect was unthinkable to Paul, who quickly added in verse 20, "But in fact Christ has been raised from the dead, the first fruits of those who have fallen asleep."

G. R. Beasley-Murray began his book *Christ Is Alive* by recounting an experience of the late Dr. W. Y. Fullerton. In a small village in Switzerland, a series of chapels had been erected, each one containing a picture showing a scene from Christ's last hours. As a pilgrim climbed the mountain from chapel to chapel, he could be reminded of Christ's path from his trial before Herod all the way to Calvary. Dr. Fullerton observed that many pilgrim feet had made a well-worn path to the chapel showing Christ on the cross. He also noted that the path seemed to lead beyond that chapel toward the summit. However, the path beyond the chapel of the crucifixion showed little evidence of having been used. Continuing on that path toward the summit, Dr. Fullerton found another shrine—the chapel of the resurrection. Those who had built the chapels had not overlooked this part of the gospel, but most of the people had stopped at Calvary.[8]

The cross is at the heart of the Christian gospel. Christians have been right to recognize this. The problem is not the well-worn path to the cross but the seldom-used path to the empty tomb. Paul gloried in the cross, but he preached the gospel of the cross in the light of the resurrection. By itself, the cross is not good news; it is defeat, not victory. Only after Christ was raised from the dead did the disciples see the meaning of the crucifixion. Only then did they see that the crucifixion was a divine victory over sin. For as Paul pointed out to the Corinthians: without the resurrection, the Christian gospel is a lie, the Christian life is a vacuum, and the Christian hope is a delusion.

The Hope of Future Resurrection (15:20–34)

The Greeks and the Hebrews had completely different concepts of the afterlife. The Hebrews could conceive of life after death only in terms of resurrection; the Greeks could conceive of life after death only if it was not in terms of resurrection. Some of the Greek philosophers and religious spokesmen taught the immortality of the soul, but none of them taught the resurrection of the body. Aeschylus expressed the typical Greek attitude toward resurrection:

" . . . when the dust hath drunk the blood of man
And he's once dead, there's no uprising."[9]

Resurrection or immortality? Those Greeks who believed in an afterlife expressed it in terms of the immortality of the soul. They believed that man by his very nature possesses an immortal soul. During life the eternal soul is imprisoned in a mortal body, but death frees the soul for continued existence. This was very likely the view of many of the Corinthian Christians: they believed in an afterlife, but they did not believe it would be a resurrection life.

Paul insisted that the future resurrection of believers is sure because of the resurrection of Jesus (vv. 1–19). The way in which Paul described the resurrection in verses 20–28 helps us contrast the Christian concept of resurrection and the Greek idea of immortality.

In verses 25–26 Paul spoke of death as an enemy, not as a friend. Sin and death are linked together in biblical thought (see Rom. 5:12). Thus man is hopelessly caught in the grip of sin and death. Only the grace and power of God can liberate man. This is the meaning of the death and resurrection of Christ. As men, we are caught in the bondage of sin and death because we have followed in the footsteps of our forefather Adam. Only as we come to be in Christ do we have the assurance that we shall be made alive (vv. 21–22). The New Testament sometimes speaks of eternal life as a present possession (see John 3:16; 5:24). In this sense we have already been made alive in Christ. However, Paul was writing about the final victory over death, of which our present experience is a foretaste.

According to the Greek view, death is a friend. The Greeks regarded immortality as an inherent part of man's nature. Little was said about man being a sinner. Man is mortal because his immortal soul is imprisoned in a corruptible body. Death is the friend who sets the soul free. Thus the Greeks based their hope of immortality on the nature of man, not on the grace and power of God. Immortality is a part of the nature of things, not the result of the grace of the life-giving God. Paul occasionally used the word "immortality," but he always used it of the life bestowed on man as a result of God's power over sin and death, shown in the resurrection of Jesus from the dead (see vv. 53–54).

Oscar Cullman has called attention to a vivid illustration of this contrast between the Christian view of death and the Greek view. He contrasts the death of Socrates as described by Plato and the death of Jesus as pictured in the New Testament.[10] Socrates had been condemned to death. When the time came, he calmly drank the poison. He died quietly, surrounded by his friends. As he died, he welcomed death because it came to separate his soul from its enemy the body.[11] By contrast, Jesus shrank from death. But he chose to grapple with this dread enemy in order to free mankind from the power of sin and death.

There is also another important contrast between immortality and resurrection. The Greek hope of immortality focused on the survival of an individual after death. The Christian hope of resurrection focuses on the fulfilment of God's purposes for his people. In verses 23–24 Paul wrote of the future resurrection in connection with Christ's final coming. This is always the biblical perspective. The Greeks focused on the individual; the Bible focuses on God and his purposes. (See vv. 27–28.)

This does not mean that an individual is unimportant or that he is absorbed into God. To the contrary, it means that the personality of a Christian reaches its goal only in relation to God and his kingdom. The Bible defines life in terms of a proper relation to God and God's people. Only in this context does a person become truly alive. Eternal life heightens and magnifies this life known now only in fore-taste. The future resurrection will be the consummation of this goal of divine redemption for his people. Thus a Christian's hope is focused not on his own survival but on the final coming of God's kingdom.

John Baillie commented on the view of J. M. E. McTaggart, an atheist who believed in the immortality of the soul. McTaggart went to great lengths to prove the immortality of the soul; he also went out of his way to deny the existence of God. He spoke of a heaven without God. Baillie said that "to speak of *heaven* without *God* is to depart entirely from the accepted meaning of the term. What McTaggart did, if he did anything, was to prove the existence of hell and the non-existence of heaven."[12] In other words, an endless existence without God *is* hell.

Practical implications. In verses 29–34 Paul raised some questions about the bearing of the doctrine of resurrection on the way people live. He insisted that Christian belief in a future resurrection is a strong motivating force for Christian living.

Verse 29 is among the most difficult verses in the New Testament. Paul wrote, "Otherwise, what do people mean by being baptized on behalf of the dead? If the dead are not raised at all, why are people baptized on their behalf?" The verse seems to indicate that the Corinthians had a practice of being baptized for those who had died, perhaps for some believers who died before being baptized. There is no other biblical reference to such a custom. Even if it existed, Paul's reference does not indicate that he approved of it. He merely used the practice to remind the Corinthians of the implicit faith in a future resurrection expressed in such a baptism.

In fact, this is true of a believer's baptism on his own profession of faith. The picture of resurrection is clearly set forth in immersion. The act depicts Christ's resurrection, our own spiritual resurrection, and the future resurrection. Possibly this is what Paul meant in verse 29. Some interpreters believe that the words translated "on behalf of the dead" can mean "with an interest in the resurrection of the dead."

Paul turned from baptism to his own experience in facing death for Christ's sake. He asked: "Why am I in peril every hour? I protest, brethren, by my pride in you which I have in Christ Jesus our Lord, I die every day" (vv. 30–31). Paul's hope was what helped him to live so thoughtlessly of his own safety and even of his own life. Without Christian hope, such self-sacrifice would be foolish, and such courage would be unlikely. But because of Christian hope, such self-sacrifice becomes the accepted pattern for Christian living and service. And Christian hope inspires a courage to defy death in the service of the Lord.

As far as Paul was concerned, Christian hope and Christian living are inseparable. "If the dead are not raised," Paul wrote in verse 32, a logical conclusion would be, " 'Let us eat and drink, for tomorrow we die.' " Paul was not stating his own view; he was setting forth the view of many in his day who lived only for the pleasures of the moment. (Similar expressions of this popular philosophy of life are found in Isa. 22:13, Eccl. 2:24, and Luke 12:19.) Adolf Deissmann refers to an ancient gravestone on which the epitaph challenges the passer-by, "Drink, for thou seest the end." Deissmann observes: "The exhortation to drink in anticipation of approaching death is one of the well-known formulae of ancient popular morals (often, no doubt of popular wit), and is by no means rare in epitaphs."[13]

Apparently there was real danger that the Corinthians would be influenced by such ideas. So Paul challenged them to avoid such people and such sins (vv. 33–34).

Some modern critics raise this question, "But what of those people with no clear hope of life to come who still live good and useful lives?" Paul's words do not deny the existence of such people. There were some in Paul's day; there are some today. Paul's point is that in the popular mind, the logical result of denying the Christian hope is a purely materialistic way of life.

Within recent years, many people have cut themselves off from the Christian faith. The ultimate results of this are seldom immediately apparent. Often such people retain Christian ideas of morality and service. They intend to preserve the "good" and "practical" parts of the Christian religion while discarding the "unbelievable" supernatural aspects of it. Outwardly, such people sometimes seem fairly successful in accomplishing their goal.

But after several generations, Christian standards begin to wither. Ours has been called a "cut-flower civilization."[14] Western society has deep roots in the Christian faith. However, for several generations many people have cut themselves off from these roots. This is like cutting a flower and putting it in a vase of water. For a while the blossoms will remain fresh and attractive, but eventually they will wither.

Modern American society contains many examples of this

withering process: The breakdown of moral standards. The crass materialism. The denial of death. The superficial level of much modern living. The absence of meaning and purpose. The loss of courage and commitment.

Paul's words in 1 Corinthians 15:30–34 lead us to view these things as logical results of people detaching themselves and their children from Christian faith and hope. The point made by Paul is still valid: the strength of Christian faith and hope is reflected in the quality of our living and serving. This faith and hope not only prepares us to die but also equips us to live. Living in the light of eternity challenges and empowers us to live life on the highest level. Like Paul we are also able to live with commitment and courage, facing the hundreds of "little deaths" that precede our actual encounter with death itself.

Victory over Death (15:35-58)

The Pharisees believed in a resurrection of flesh and blood bodies. The Sadducees believed in no kind of life after death. Therefore, the Sadducees took delight in posing difficult questions about the nature of the resurrection. One of their questions concerned a woman widowed seven times. They asked Jesus the same question that doubtlessly had stumped the Pharisees, " 'In the resurrection . . . whose wife will the woman be?' " (Luke 20:33.) The answer of Jesus affirmed the future resurrection but not under flesh and blood conditions of earthly life. (See Luke 20: 34–38.)

The resurrection body. Paul knew that the Corinthians had what they thought were unanswerable objections to the resurrection. The fact of the physical body's decomposition seems to rule out any possibility of resurrection of the body. This objection is implied in their questions to Paul: " 'How are the dead raised? With what kind of body do they come?' " Paul's answer to these questions followed the same general direction as Jesus' answer to the Sadducees. On one hand, Paul avoided the Pharisees' concept of a flesh and blood resurrection. On the other hand, he affirmed a biblical view of resurrection, not a Greek view of immortality.

Paul said plainly, "Flesh and blood cannot inherit the kingdom of God, nor does the perishable inherit the imperishable" (v. 50). This might seem to rule out a bodily resurrection, but Paul held to his concept of resurrection. He explained that he was talking about resurrection of the body, but not resuscitation of the physical body.

The apostle used the analogy of a seed and a plant (vv. 36–38). Raymond Bryan Brown points out that care should be taken in interpreting this analogy. Paul was not writing as a botanist who is describing the inherent power of germination in the seed. "He means that a seed is buried, and something different, a plant comes from it. A human body is buried and in the resurrection it becomes another kind of body. Paul is not emphasizing continuity at this point but difference. You plant one thing and something else comes up."[15]

In verses 39–41 the apostle stressed that all flesh and all kinds of bodies are not the same kind. His point is that since God already has created so many different kinds of bodies, he is fully capable of even more glorious acts of creation, such as the creation of the resurrection body.

Paul referred to this resurrection body as a "spiritual body." In verses 42–44 he spelled out the contrasts between this glorious spiritual body and the perishable physical body. In verses 45–49 he contrasted the physical bodies of men who are descendants of Adam with the spiritual bodies that will be given to those being transformed into the image of Christ. "A spiritual body is one that is made vital by the Spirit and fit to be in the presence of God in the age to come. A physical body is appropriate in this present age; a spiritual body will be appropriate in the age to come."[16]

Paul's concept of a spiritual body is very close to what we mean by personality. The spiritual body will be the completed state of God's redeeming work. The total personality of a believer will be fully redeemed as a part of God's total redemption of the universe (see Rom. 8:18–23). The redeemed body will be comparable to the new heavens and earth of the future age.

As noted earlier, the biblical focus of attention is not on the survival of an individual beyond death, but on the fulfilment of God's redemptive work. A believer's personality will be fully redeemed in relation to God's fulfilled purpose. He will become himself as God intends for him to be when he finds his proper place in relation to God and his redeemed brothers. Thus the resurrection of believer's body takes place in connection with the final redemption of the body of Christ. "Resurrection means that *all the person* will be redeemed when *all the people of God* are redeemed."[17]

Thanks be to God. In 1 Corinthians 15, Paul was not attempting to write a complete treatment of the doctrine of life after death. He was seeking to deal with a specific set of problems in the Corinthian church. Therefore, he did not answer all our questions about life after death. For example, he did not deal with the state of the dead prior to the resurrection.

He did refer on several occasions to dead Christians as those *fallen asleep in Christ* (vv. 18, 20, 51). Although some Christians have interpreted this to mean that the spirits of the dead are in a state of passive slumber, most Christians have seen "sleep" as an analogy to describe how the dead appear to those who are still alive. In 1 Thessalonians 4:13–14, Paul referred to those who have fallen asleep as being with Christ and as coming with Christ when he returns. In

Philippians 1:21–23, Paul referred to his own hope of departing at death to be with Christ.

Just as there are many unanswered questions about the nature of the future resurrection body, so there are many unanswered questions about the nature of the present state of the dead in Christ. But this much seems clear: (1) Whatever their state, they are with Christ. (2) They too await the final resurrection of the body. (3) When Christ returns, the dead in Christ will return with him. (4) At that time the dead in Christ and those believers still living will receive transformed, resurrected bodies.

This latter point is forcefully made in 1 Corinthians 15: 51–57. These verses celebrate the final victory over death mentioned earlier in verses 25–26. In lyrical language Paul wrote:

" 'O death, where is thy victory?
O death, where is thy sting?'

The sting of death is sin, and the power of sin is the law. But thanks be to God, who gives us the victory through our Lord Jesus Christ" (vv. 55–57) .

This victorious hymn of praise is based on something more basic than Paul's ability to describe in detail the nature of life after death. One of Paul's interpreters makes this wise observation: "In his teaching about the Last Things Paul is aware that 'we know only in part,' that our present knowledge is very much like vision through an unclear mirror. That complete redemption awaits all those who are 'in Christ' he is sure, as that God will finally 'be all in all.' Beyond this he does not go. A strong faith, it has been said, is not curious about details. It is enough to know that 'this perishable nature must put on the imperishable, and this mortal nature must put on immortality (1 Cor. 15: 53) .' For the rest, 'eye hath not seen, nor ear heard, neither have entered into the heart of man the things which God hath prepared for them that love him. (1 Cor. 2:9).' "[18]

Paul's confident hope was based on his faith in the resurrection of Christ, which included his experience of the prescence of the Spirit of the risen Lord. Because of this, Paul spoke as if the future victory over death had already taken place. A man gave this evaluation of a famous Christian teacher and preacher: " ' . . . he made me feel that tomorrow had already happened.' "[19]

The teacher had been able to convey something of the spirit of the New Testament. The writers of the New Testament wrote as if the bright tomorrow of God's purpose already had taken place. They did not look ahead wistfully, hoping against hope that the future would be bright. Theirs was the confidence of men who spoke as if the future had already happened. They were certain that Christ's incarnate victory over sin and death contained the sure promise of God's final victory.

This kind of hope makes it unnecessary to *deny* death's reality. Like Paul we can actually *defy* death. This is not because death is not a fearful enemy. Rather it is because Christ has taken the sting out of death. Because death has been robbed of its terror, a Christian can live with confidence, courage, and commitment.

Eugene O'Neill captured something of this spirit in his imaginative drama *Lazarus Laughed.* The story focuses on Lazarus of Bethany after he had been delivered from death's hold. After his encounter with death, Lazarus said: "Laugh! Laugh with me! Death is dead! Fear is no more! There is only life! There is only laughter!"[20] Later Lazarus was confronted by Caligula, the cruel heir to the Roman throne. Caligula took great delight in the power that was his because of man's fear of death. However, attempts to frighten Lazarus with the fear of death were met with laughter. Lazarus explained, "Death is dead, Caligula."[21]

Notes

Unless otherwise indicated, all Bible quotations are from the Revised Standard Version.

Chapter One

[1] *Help! I'm a Layman* (Waco, Texas: Word Books, 1966), p. 52.

[2] James W. Angell, *Put Your Arms Around the City* (Old Tappan, New Jersey: Fleming H. Revell Company), pp. 29–30.

[3] S. Angus, *The Environment of Early Christianity* (New York: Charles Schibner's Sons, 1914), p. 36.

[4] George A. Buttrick, *God, Pain, and Evil* (Nashville: Abingdon Press, 1966), p. 130.

[5] Angell, *op. cit.*, p. 29.

[6] William Baird, *The Corinthian Church—a Biblical Approach to Urban Culture* (Nashville: Abingdon Press, 1964), p. 23.

[7] *Ibid.*

[8] *Mandate to Witness* (Valley Forge, Pa: The Judson Press, 1964), p. 19.

Chapter Two

[1] Douglas MacArthur, *Reminiscences* (New York: McGraw-Hill Book Company, 1964), p. 276.

[2] Carl Sandburg, *Abraham Lincoln, The Prairie Years,* Vol. 2 (New York: Harcourt, Brace and Company, 1926), p. 306.

[3] C. S. Lewis, *Mere Christianity* (New York: The Macmillan Co., 1963), p. 94.

[4] *Ibid.*, p. 97

[5] *Ibid.*, p. 95.

[6] Jack Finegan, *Light from the Ancient Past,* second edition (Princeton, New Jersey: Princeton University Press, 1959), p. 373.

[7] J. Stanley Glen, *Pastoral Problems in First Corinthians* (Philadelphia: Westminster Press, 1964), p. 35.

[8] J. Ralph Grant, *The Way of the Cross* (Grand Rapids, Michigan: Baker Book House, 1963), p. 26.

[9] Quoted by Origen, *Contra Celsum* III, 44. Translated with an intro-

duction and notes by Henry Chadwick. (Cambridge: At the University Press, 1953), p. 158.

10 Leslie D. Weatherhead, *Key Next Door* (Nashville: Abingdon Press, 1960), p. 127.

11 Quoted by Paul W. Hoor, "On Getting Along Without Religion," *Survey*, March, 1963, p. 24.

12 *Ibid.*

13 C. R. Daley, Jr., "Spiritual Retardation Among Baptists," *Western Recorder*, September 28, 1967, p. 4.

14 Wayne Dehoney, "Keeping Your Religion Up to Date," *Survey*, July, 1963, p. 6.

15 Raymond B. Brown, *The Broadman Bible Commentary*, Vol. 10 (Nashville: Broadman Press, 1970), p. 315.

16 Quoted by Halford E. Luccock, *The Haunted House and Other Sermons* (New York: The Abingdon Press, 1923), p. 199.

17 Gerald Kennedy, *The Parables* (New York: Harper and Brothers, Publishers, 1960), pp. 126–127.

18 William Hull, "The Hidden Persuaders," *Survey*, June, 1962, p. 36.

Chapter Three

1 Pitirim Sorokin, *The American Sex Revolution* (Boston: Porter Sargent Publisher, 1956), pp. 3–4.

2 See David Mace, *The Christian Response to the Sexual Revolution* (Nashville: Abingdon Press, 1970), p. 68.

3 Lester A. Kirkendall and Elizabeth Ogg, *Sex and Our Society*, Public Affairs Pamphlet No. 366. (Public Affairs Committee, Inc., 1964), pp. 8–9.

4 See *The Sexual Wilderness* (New York: David McKay Company, Inc., 1968), p. 17.

5 John W. Drakeford, *The Great Sex Swindle* (Nashville: Broadman Press, 1966), p. 34.

6 Mace, *op. cit.*, p. 93.

7 *Ibid.*, pp. 94–95.

8 Raymond B. Brown, *The Broadman Bible Commentary*, Vol. 10 (Nashville: Broadman Press, 1970), p. 320.

9 Mace, *op. cit.*, p. 126.

10 John Cuber, "How New Ideas About Sex Are Changing Our Lives," *Redbook*, March, 1971, p. 176.

11 Drakeford, *op. cit.*, pp. 36–37.

12 Quoted by Anson Mount, public affairs director of *Playboy*, in *Baptist Press* release, March 18, 1970.

13 Brown, *op. cit.*, p. 326

14 New York: Harper and Row Publishers, 1952, p. 44.

15 *Ibid.*, p. 53.

[16] *Pulpit Digest,* September, 1966, p. 44.

[17] Norman Vincent Peale, "Man, Morals, and Maturity," *Reader's Digest,* October, 1965, p. 275.

[18] *The Secular City,* revised edition (New York: The Macmillan Company, 1966), p. 177.

[19] C. S. Lewis, *The Screwtape Letters* (London: The Centenary Press, 1942), p. 49.

[20] *The First Epistle of Paul to the Corinthians* (New York: Harper and Brothers, Publishers, *n. d.*), p. 98.

[21] Evelyn Duvall, *Why Wait Till Marriage?* (New York: Association Press, 1965), p. 90.

[22] Peale, *op. cit.,* pp. 275–276.

Chapter Four

[1] See Milton Rokeach, "Persuasion That Persists," *Psychology Today.* September, 1971, p. 70.

[2] In *Nation Under God.* Edited by Fances Brentano, revised and enlarged edition. (Clinton, Mass.: The Colonial Press Inc., 1964), p. 92.

[3] Paul Geren, *Burma Diary* (New York: Harper and Brothers, 1943), pp. 51–52.

[4] *The First Epistle of Paul to the Corinthians* (New York: Harper and Brothers Publishers, *n. d.*), pp. 123–124.

[5] Quoted by J. D. Jones, *Watching the Cross* (Garden City, New York: Doubleday, Doran and Company, Inc., 1928), p. 296.

[6] Richard Collier, *The General Next to God* (New York: E. P. Dutton and Co., Inc., 1965), p. 215.

[7] Leslie Weatherhead, *Key Next Door* (Nashville: Abingdon Press, 1960), p. 199.

[8] Walter Lord, *A Night to Remember* (New York: Holt, Rinehart and Winston, 1955), p. 38.

[9] Weatherhead, *op. cit.,* p. 200.

[10] *Ibid.,* p. 198.

[11] *The Freedom of the Christian Man* (New York: Harper and Row, Publishers, 1963), p. 28.

Chapter Five

[1] Dwight Whitney, "Squire of Cave Creek," *TV Guide,* October 9, 1971, p. 34.

[2] E. Stanley Jones, *The Reconstruction of the Church—On What Pattern?* (New York: Abingdon Press, 1970), pp. 11–12.

[3] Elton Trueblood, *The Incendiary Fellowship* (New York: Harper and Row, Publisher, 1967), p. 9.

[4] *Ibid.,* pp. 85–86.

[5] William Barclay, *The Letters to the Corinthians,* Second edition (Philadelphia: The Westminster Press, 1956), p. 116.

6 J. Stanley Glen, *Pastoral Problems in First Corinthians* (Philadelphia: The Westminster Press, 1964), p. 149.

7 John Short, "The First Epistle to the Corinthians" (Exposition), *The Interpreter's Bible*, Vol. 10 (New York: Abingdon Press, 1953), p. 132.

8 Helmut Thielicke, *The Waiting Father*, Translated by John W. Doberstein (New York: Harper and Row, Publishers, 1959), p. 107.

9 See Thomas J. Fleming, *One Small Candle* (New York: W. W. Norton and Co., Inc., 1964), p. 153

10 Grady Cothen, "Southern Baptists and a Declining America," *Home Missions*, August, 1963, p. 19.

11 See David Wilkerson, *The Cross and the Switchblade* (Westwood, New Jersey: Fleming H. Revell Company, 1963), p. 159.

12 Frank Stagg, E. Glenn Hinson, and Wayne Oates, *Glossolalia: Tongue Speaking in Biblical, Historical, and Psychological Perspective* (Nashville: Abingdon Press, 1967), p. 37.

13 Jones, *op. cit.*, p. 137.

14 Findley B. Edge, *A Quest for Vitality in Religion* (Nashville: Broadman Press, 1963), pp. 22–23.

Chapter Six

1 See Elisabeth Kübler-Ross, *On Death and Dying* (New York: The Macmillan Company, 1969).

2 "Go Down Death" in *A Man Called Peter* by Catherine Marshall, (New York: McGraw-Hill Book Co., Inc., 1951), pp. 266–267.

3 Liston O. Mills, ed., *Perspectives on Death* (New York: Abingdon Press, 1969), pp. 7–8.

4 C. K. Barrett, *The First Epistle to the Corinthians* (New York: Harper and Row, Publishers, 1968), p. 340.

5 Hugh J. Schonfield, *The Passover Plot* (New York: Bernard Geis associates, 1965), pp. 158–181.

6 Robert James Dean, "A Study of *ELPIS* in the New Testament," An unpublished dissertation. New Orleans Baptist Theological Seminary, 1961, pp. 161–162.

7 James Moffatt, *The First Epistle of Paul to the Corinthians* (New York: Harper and Brothers, Publishers, *n. d.*), p. 242.

8 G. R. Beasley-Murray, *Christ Is Alive* (London: Lutterworth Press, 1947), pp. 11–12.

9 Aeschylus, *Eumenides*, 647–648, *The Plays of Aeschylus* in *Great Books of the Western World*, Vol. 5 (Chicago: Encyclopedia Britannica, Inc., 1952), p. 88.

10 Oscar Cullman, *Immortality of the Soul or Resurrection of the Dead?* (London: The Epworth Press, 1958), pp. 19–27.

11 Plato, *Phaedo*, 64A–68B.

[12] John Baillie, *And the Life Everlasting* (New York: Charles Scribner's Sons, 1933), p. 113.

[13] Adolf Deissmann, *Light from the Ancient East,* translated by Lionel R. M. Strachan (New York: George H. Doran Company, 1927), p. 295.

[14] Elton Trueblood, *The Predicament of Modern Man* (New York: Harper and Brothers, Publishers, 1944), p. 59.

[15] Raymond B. Brown, *The Broadman Bible Commentary,* Vol. 10 (Nashville: Broadman Press, 1970), p. 391.

[16] *Ibid.*

[17] Dean, *op. cit.,* p. 196.

[18] Archibald M. Hunter, *The Gospel According to Paul* (Philadelphia: The Westminster Press, 1966), pp. 56–57.

[19] Michael Sadler referring to Karl Barth. Quoted by J. S. Whale, *Victor and Victim* (Cambridge: At the University Press, 1960), p. 16.

[20] Eugene O'Neill, *Lazarus Laughed* (New York: Horace Leveright, 1927), p. 23.

[21] *Ibid.,* p. 69.